THANKSGIVING AND PRAISE

OTHER BOOKS BY

Mark Gruber, O.S.B.
in collaboration with
M. Michele Ransil, C.D.P.

Wounded by Love: Intimations of an Outpouring Heart

Exalted in Glory: Encountering the Risen Christ

Waiting for Dawn: Portents of His Coming

THANKSGIVING AND PRAISE

Dandelions for God

Mark Gruber, O.S.B.

in collaboration with

M. Michele Ransil, C.D.P.

Foreword by Mike Aquilina
Editor of *New Covenant*

St. Vincent Spirituality Publications
Saint Vincent Archabbey
Latrobe, Pennsylvania

Imprimi Potest: Rt. Rev. Douglas R. Nowicki, O.S.B.
Archabbot, Saint Vincent Archabbey,
Latrobe, Pennsylvania

Cover design by David Camaione

Unless otherwise noted, Scripture passages are taken from *The New American Bible* of the Confraternity of Christian Doctrine, Washington, D.C., ©1970.

Printed in the United States of America

IBSN 1-886565-06-6

To the Vicar of Christ,
our beloved Holy Father, Pope John Paul II,
in gratitude for:

° his tremendous zeal in proclaiming the Good News of the Gospel;

° his unflinching courage in upholding the teachings and traditions of our Catholic faith;

° his profound appreciation of the role of the Virgin Mary in the life of the Church;

° his unceasing defense of the sanctity of all human life, those born and unborn;

° his promulgation of the gift of marriage and family life as an aspect of Trinitarian and Paschal spirituality;

° his deep compassion for the poor, the homeless and the victims of violence and natural disasters;

° his fearless denunciation of the evils of materialism and our secular culture; and

° his tireless efforts in promoting a just and lasting world peace.

My vows to thee I will perform,
O God;
I will render offerings of thanks
to thee,
For thou hast delivered my soul
from death,
and my feet from stumbling,
that I may walk before God
in the light of the living.
cf. Psalm 56:12-13

For who has known the mind of
the Lord?
Or who has been his counselor?
Who has given him anything so
as to deserve return?
For from him and through him
and for him all things are.
To him be glory forever. Amen.
Romans 11:34-36

TABLE OF CONTENTS

FOREWORD

A few years back, I had the singular privilege of being paid to read thousands of pages of the documents of early Christianity. I pored over volumes of the homilies, letters, histories, poems, theology, philosophy, and social commentary of the men we call "the Fathers of the Church."

Reading the Fathers was a powerful experience for me-- much more than an academic exercise. Before I'd finished a dozen pages, I felt transported, over centuries, to a time when Christian faith was fresh . . . when a page of the Bible was something to be savored . . . when ordinary men, women, and children were willing to die rather than stay home from a Sunday liturgy.

In all the Fathers, there was a fire burning, and it blazed across the millennia to consume my heart. It was more than eloquence--though they were eloquent. It was more than zeal--though they were zealous. It was more than erudition--though they were learned men.

It was a divine fire.

I recognized this quality at once, because I had known it before: in the conversation and preaching of Father Mark Gruber.

Now, as I read the pages of *Thanksgiving and Praise*, I feel that fire once again. Yet I cannot call Father Gruber's meditations "old-fashioned." For he is clearly our contemporary at this turn of the millennium. Like the ancient Fathers, the author of this book has taken all that is good in his native culture--in its literature, arts, and sciences--and placed it on the altar.

Father Gruber is one of us. Yet he is also one with Justin, Clement, Augustine, and Benedict. He is a genuine Father for our Church, speaking a Gospel that is ever fresh, speaking a faith worth dying for.

Mike Aquilina
Feast of St. Jerome
September 30, 1999

PREFACE

Like the three books which have preceded this one, *Thanksgiving and Praise* is a transcription of the conferences presented during a week-long Retreat which has subsequently been formatted to reproduce the cadence of the spoken word. To obtain the greatest benefit from these meditations, the reader is therefore advised to slowly "listen" to the text, rather than attempt to hastily read it in a few hours.

We are greatly indebted to Kerry Crawford and to Father Mark Wenzinger, O.S.B., not only for their willingness to undertake the task of proofreading the text, but also for their insightful comments on its contents.

INTRODUCTION

The union with God for which we were created (and re-created in Christ) begins in this world when we pray. The vision of God for which the eyes of our heart were made to behold is the beatific end of this life which we already glimpse in the worship of prayer. Prayer is as much God's outpouring of love upon us as our aspiration to commune with him, and the grace of it is pervasive to the human condition. There never was a person who "didn't have a prayer" because there never was an ungenerous moment in God. Moreover, there are many prayers which rise up from the inmost recesses of the human heart of which the doubting mind has little knowledge and the tongue has even less participation.

Prayers of praise and thanksgiving to God are more often among the latter kind than many believers would suppose. We naturally tend to petition God, but we feel that gratitude emerges only from a sense of obligation. While it is true that justice requires gratitude from us in prayer and that a well-formed conscience can impose the responsibility of thanksgiving on the soul, it is no less certain that a fully alive soul will spontaneously offer prayers of praise and thanksgiving to God by the merest exercise of the senses in a world infused with grace and beauty.

This outpouring is an exercise of bliss which leads us towards the beatific vision and divine union. In its purest moments, we are transported from our ordinary occupation of time, space and bodily form. Christians do not speak so much about this transport in terms of escaping the flesh, but of occupying it for once in peace. Certain limits imposed upon life from its inherent insecurities and tensions of external stress seem to melt away. Moses was rapt in prayer for forty days and forty nights without food or sleep but emerged, not disembodied, but radiant of flesh. The gift of prayer is more often conjoined with the tentative emergence of the self in the midst of all its insecurities. In that case, the joys of praise and thanks-giving are limited to the trust given to God, and the needs which become our petitionary prayer receive proportionately greater emphasis.

This book is intended to aid the reader in capturing the sense of joy which attends the exercise of prayerful gratitude. The occasional release of spontaneous bursts of prayer offered as so many simple gifts to God and symbolized by the dandelions presented by a small child, are a profoundly important aspect of the spiritual life as the "gift-exchange economy" of our salvation. It is hoped that by noting the deep joy experienced in the offering of praise and thanksgiving and by seeing in the exercise of such prayer a greater openness to receive God's ever-present blessings, readers will be encouraged to embrace the grace of divine praise and the human impulse of true thanksgiving more fully. In doing so, the Eucharistic work of Jesus will be extended and they will be immersed more fully into the prayer which Christ always offers to his Eternal Father.

Feast of St. Augustine
August 28, 1999

I

The Philosophical Attitude

When I first entered college,
I enrolled as a history major.

It was an interest of my family.

My grandfather,
for instance,
had always given me history books to read,
and I enjoyed them.

But sometime during my sophomore year,
I was required to take a philosophy course.
On the first day of class,
the professor asked us to pause a moment
                    and to ask ourselves this question:

"Why is it
            that this world *is*?
  Why is there this world
                when it would be simpler,
                            more economical
  if this world were not?"

Most of my classmates rolled their eyes
                        into the back of their head.
There was an audible groan
                from the back of the room.

Some students sighed;
others looked absent-mindedly
                    out the window.

But I was hooked.

After the class was over that afternoon,
I went straight to the Registrar's Office
        and changed my major
to philosophy.

Because the question which the professor asked:
        "Why is it that this world *is*?"
                    is
after all,
the most important question
                    for the exercise
of the human mind.

Maybe there are more important questions
                        for the human heart.
Maybe there are more important questions
                        for day-to-day survival,
but the senses of the mind
are constantly engaged
                by the wonder
that there *is* a world,
that there is a *self*
                in the midst of the world.

If we consider
        that this is just too tedious a mind game
to play,
it is only
        that we have forgotten our original interest
when we were first introduced
to the sensible world.

For rising up within us
        that question--
                        maybe not in concrete terms,
                        maybe not in explicit words,
  but that question was evoked in us
                        with every sensation
in the earliest moments
of our lives.

"Why, O why?"

This is not just an academic question.
The "why" of being
is a question
        which seeks the foundation
                        of the meaning of the world,
the meaning of life.

The question was not at first
                        an intellectual exercise.
Philosophers came along later and claimed it;
        they elaborated it;
        they embellished it.

5

But before there was ever a philosopher,
a baby
          was already immersed in the question,
                    and pondered it
day and night.

A fair elaboration of the philosophy of Plato
would suggest
that a newborn babe in a crib
                    is more pure of mind,
                              more attuned to reality
and is,
therefore,
          more readily consumed
by the question
                    "Why?"

Plato thought
that each soul pre-existed,
                    contemplating eternal truths.
He believed
that birth brings forgetfulness
and as we grow older,
                    if we are not careful,
we become hardened;
we become duller.

We forget our original wisdom
and so
we neglect the awe and the wonder
                    of our existence.

As we grow older
we can grow more distant from the basic issue,
                    the deepest meaning of life.

We lose track of our original interest,
the foundational fascination
with life.

When we no longer think of the question "Why?"
we will have forgotten
                    who we are
                    and where we have come from.
We become a shadow of ourselves.

The basic philosophical question
                    of "Why?"
is the antidote
to the prevailing secular attitude
which has no more wonder in this world,
          and no more wonder
                              of this world.

The philosophical mind says,
          "Why, O why?"

The secular mind says,
          "So what?"

"So what" is the attitude of the hardened
                              and the cynical.

7

With each experience that comes along,
      they look at it and say:
          "Seen it,
          heard it,
          thought it,
            did it."
And they dismiss it.

For the contemporary secular mind,
      there is nothing new under the sun.

The age-old philosophical question
dissipated and spent itself
till it has not even the strength
          of vigorous doubt.
For them,
     all is *blasé*;
     the whole world is tedious.

For the spiritual mind,
the classical philosophical question
has been graced with greater poignancy
          and clarity.
For them,
     everything is *new* under the sun.

Every bush is burning as a revelation,
every experience
        is an opportunity of gratitude,
          and beyond gratitude,
it is an occasion of grace.

8

The recovery of wonder,
the recovery of questioning "Why?"
is a basic spiritual exercise
for us.

It is not the same question that the scientist asks.

The scientist asks the question,
        "How, O how?"

The scientist wants to know
        how things originated,
        how things work,
        how they operate
                moment by moment.
The scientist wants to understand
        by what mechanism
                the material processes unfold.
The scientist is interested
        in the interrelationship
of the parts.

The philosopher marvels over the fact
                that the whole even exists at all.

We live in an age
in which people think
        that science can answer all our questions.
But science can't even answer all the questions
                about "how!"

Science can answer exactly *nothing* about "why!"

It is a conviction of our Faith
that the question about "why"
is a bigger question,
and a deeper question
than the question about "how."

It is the conviction of our Faith
that,
    ultimately,
               the question of "why"
even answers the question of "how."

It is a revealed truth
that,
    in the beginning,
God created the universe.
It is God who sustains it;
it is God who completes and perfects it.

The question "Why?" is a question about seeking God.

Very often
the question "how"
is too distracted
to seek God.

As people of faith,
we must also deal with the questions
                              of how
                              and what
                              and where
                              and when.
But none of these questions
will ever replace the deeper,
                    spiritual quest
of seeking God.

Alas,
when we ask "Why?" in the course of our lives,
it is usually a lament,
          and a complaint.

We only ask the question
              when everything has gone wrong,
              when all of the how's and how-to's
have failed
and we can no longer manage
              and control our lives.

We don't really ask "Why?"
              in wonder of the miracle of creation.

We don't really ask "Why?"
              in the wonder of sensation.

We only ask "Why?"
              when things break down.

"Why can I not stay in control?"
"Why is this being taken from me?"

For many people,
this question "Why?"
            is not the deeper one of wonder;
        it is not the one
                    which ends in thanksgiving
and praise.

It is a dangerous thing
        to ask hard questions
        outside the experience
of wonder and praise.

It is a dangerous thing
        to be analyzing,
                surveying,
                grappling
        and wrestling with the world
when there is no gratitude in our heart.

We will likely stumble and fall,
                lose hope,
                become disheartened
and despair.

We ought not to ask the question,
        "Why is everything in the world going wrong?"
unless we have a strong foundation
for asking the question,
        "Why do I believe in a world going right?"
or even,
        "Why is there a world at all?"

Why is there green grass
                    on *either* side of the fence?
Why are there blue skies and white clouds?
Why is there the gentle rain
                    or falling snow?
Why is it
        that I have the flesh to feel
                        the warmth of fire,
                        the coldness of ice?
                        the texture of wood,
                        the soft summer breeze?

Why am I here?
Why are you there?

Why is our life present here
                when we did not make it;
                when we could not have caused it;
                when our parents and our society
cannot explain the mystery of it?

The question, "Why, O why?"
must provide the continuous energy
                that inspires our praise
and our thanksgiving.

It was Jesus
        who taught his disciples such a mentality
when he said to them:

        "Consider the lilies of the field.
        They do not spin, neither do they weave."
                            cf. Luke 12:27

13

Consider them.

Christ didn't mean this
                just as an object lesson in botany.

He was giving them a devotional life,
                                a spirituality--
maybe not yet the whole of a devotional life;
maybe not yet the whole of Christian spirituality,
but he was giving them something
foundational.

Consider the lilies of the field.

Even Solomon in all his glory--
Solomon who was king,
                who was in charge of armies,
Solomon who was the wisest man of his age--
was not arrayed
                so beautifully
as one of these.

Jesus taught some of his greatest lessons
                        when inviting his disciples
to wonder.
                "Consider the birds of the air.
                They do not sow, neither do they reap."
                                cf. Luke 12:24

14

The birds are not in charge
of an agricultural complex;
they're not completely absorbed
                              in the tedium of life.
The question of "how" does not overwhelm them.

They are gathered up into the sweep
                    of the creative work of God.

Jesus invited his disciples
to observe the world around them--
            not so much as scientists,
                    but as philosophers
                        or poets
because the philosophical question,
            the poetic question,
is a greater question,
    a deeper question,
and foundational
to any other question
about creation.

All of the "hows" of creation
                    are secondary;
the "why" is primary.

The vocation to gratitude
is the original vocation
            of our human race.

15

When Adam and Eve were created,
                    they were created in a garden.
The garden was called "Eden"--
which in Hebrew means
                    "a fertile valley."
It was probably the flood plain of a river,
                    perhaps the delta of Egypt,
or the Tigris and Euphrates
                              of Mesopotamia
or the Gihon of Ethiopia.

In ancient Biblical days
the flood plains of the Near East
were laden with palm trees and vines,
                    pomegranates,
                    ferns,
                and flowers.
They were veritable gardens.

The word "Eden" has a secondary meaning.
It also means "delight,"
and so we call the Garden of Eden,
                "the Garden of Delight."

Our first parents were created
to do nothing more
          than to spend their days
                              in sheer delight,
feasting their eyes on the beauty of creation
and to wonder
                "Why, O why?"

The question would gradually resolve itself
                    in praise and thanksgiving
as slowly but surely,
they would begin to understand
that all of it
                was a gift.

It wasn't an accident;
it was created for them to enjoy,
                    to cherish
                    and to cultivate--
like a garden.

Their hearts would likewise be cultivated
                    from wonder to delight
                    from delight
to thanksgiving.

This was the original design.

The delights
which God planted in the garden
                    for Adam and Eve
were intended to gradually win them,
                    to gently call them outside of themselves
until they could live in perfect mutuality
with him.

There were two special gifts
                    which God placed in the garden.

In time,
when they had grown and matured
                        toward union with him,
he was going to give them
the fruit of two trees.

Just as a young couple
might see in the garden of their courtship--
            in time,
                eventually,
as their love matures,
the possibility of a banquet:
                    a deep intimacy
and union.

This would not occur right away,
but the trees would be planted
to give them courage to go on,
                patience to continue the journey
                            to walk with God
along the way of their courtship
until union would be realistic,
                    and possible;
until the opportunity would be provided
by the readiness of their souls.

We know what Adam and Eve did.

In their laziness to walk the journey
                step-by-step,
                    from delight to delight,
                    from grace to grace,
                    from glory to glory,
they stole the fruit of the first tree.

18

They attempted to steal the benefits
                of union with God
before they had developed a fully honest
                        and true relationship
with him.

Young men and women often do the same thing.

They steal the benefits of intimacy
without the bond having matured
between them.

All of us do such things.

When we are too impatient with the course of our life
and want *now*
                that which satisfies us,
we complain to God
                about his pace
                  and his time
                  and his measure of the seasons.
We continually distrust God
and want now
what he has reserved for another time
                        and another season.

If Adam and Eve had taken time to be more grateful
and to fully delight
                in the gifts of God at hand,
they would have been more patient
                        to wait for the gifts
which were yet to come.

Like our first parents,
we, too, are impatient with so many people
                          and so many situations.
We are not praising and thanking God
for the gifts that we already have.

Perhaps we are only asking
              how to fix what is broken,
              how to negotiate what is problematic,
              how to resolve what is difficult.

Maybe we are preoccupying ourselves
              with the shallower questions,
and not allowing ourselves
to explore the deeper question
              which leads to wonder
and to praise.

Consider the story of Job.
In his lifetime,
      he was beset by every kind of difficulty.

His fortunes were reversed.

God struck the foundations of his house;
              the pillars collapsed
and he lost his family.

A lifelong business was destroyed;
              his body was covered with sores,
                  and he was afflicted
with great and chronic pain.

He lost control of his world.
He lost control of his home,
    lost control of his work.
He lost control of himself
        and of his body.
He was beset
        by the threat of the question,
                    the lament,
                    the despairing:
        "Why?"

This was the temptation of Job.

As chapter after chapter of the book unfolds,
his former friends came
        and made the question ever more bitter.

Even his wife said to him:
    "What use is your life? Curse God and die."
                                cf. Job 2:9

But before Job despaired,
God visited him out of the whirlwind and said:
    "Gird up your loins now, like a man."
                                Job 38:3

This is an idiom in Hebrew which means:
        "Get ready for a walk, for a journey."

And where did God take Job on that journey?
Right through creation.

God said to Job:

"Where were you when I laid out the heavens, Job?
Do you know how many stars there are?
Can you count them?

Where were you when I poured out the foundations
        of the deep?
Are your footprints down there?
Do you know how many fish there are?
Tell me, if you can.

Where were you when I founded the earth?
Who determined its size?
Tell me, if you know.
Who stretched out the measuring lines for it?
Who laid its cornerstone?
Were you there?

Do you know the courses of the birds that fly?
Have you watched them from above?
Does the eagle fly at your command
To build its nest on the cliff-top?"

In line after line,
verse after verse,
God said to Job:
                "Look,
                 ponder,
                 consider,
                 reflect.
"Walk through creation, O Job,
 and ask yourself greater questions
                        than before."

And in the end, Job said to God:

> *"I have dealt with great things that I*
> *do not understand*
> *things too wonderful for me,*
> *which I cannot know.*
> *I had heard of you by word of mouth,*
> *but now my eye has seen you.*
> *Therefore I disown what I have said,*
> *and repent in dust and ashes."*
>
> Job 42:3-6

Job repented
because in seeing the works of creation--
                the very works
                            which Adam had overlooked--
his senses became alive to their beauty.

He stood in awe and wonder
                at the power and goodness of God.

Job had seen these works all his life,
but before his walk with God
he saw creation
                as something to be exploited for his own gain,
                something he could manage and control
for his own benefit.

He saw it first
                as opportunity
                or obstacle
                or indifferent matter,
but now he saw it
                as coming from the hand of God.

Before any of Job's fortunes were reversed,
before any of his wealth was returned,
before any of his family was replaced,
before any of his health was restored
                    Job was at peace
because he was able to perceive these benefits
                    as the works of God,
                        the gifts of God.

He was able to live in wonder and heartfelt praise;
he was able to live in the original innocence
                                of thanksgiving
in a world which was still,
            after all,
the Eden of God's handiwork.

This is also our call; this must also be our vocation.

We should try to see all things
                    as blessings and gifts
before we see them
                    as problems and difficulties.

Did you pass through the season of Spring
                    with allergies?
Maybe you forgot to think about dust and pollen
                        as a sign of the indomitable presence
of God's creative Providence.

24

Pollen is a sign
            that the ongoing work of creation
is well done,
            down to the finest microscopic detail.
Dust is proof
            that the whole world is spinning around
                        right under our noses
causing us to respond physically
            with the full force of our lungs
and thereby to acknowledge
that it is there.

While we are sneezing
            and coughing
            and weeping,
are we marvelling at the fine print
in the Book of Creation?

When we are suffering
            in the oppressive heat of summer,
can we look at the sun
and marvel at the power of God
            which dims a thousand suns?

Can we marvel at the light of Christ
            who shone in his Transfiguration
more brilliantly than the sun?

When we are drenched with perspiration,
can we say of the humidity,
            "Bless the Lord, O my soul"?

Can we say of the lines around our eyes--
the signs of age--

       "Bless the Lord, O my soul"?

Can we look at the latest gray hair,
the deeper furrow in our brow and say,

       "Bless the Lord, O my soul"?

Can we join our voices to the three youths
       in the fiery furnace?
Can we sing:

    "Aches and pains,
       give glory and eternal praise to him.
    "Scuff and stain,
       bless the Lord.
    "Mold and mildew,
       bless the Lord;
       give glory and eternal praise to him."

When we were babies,
we marveled at mold and mud,
       at mildew and dust;
we marveled at dandelions.

When we were children,
we marveled at the gray hairs of our grandparents
       and the wrinkles in their faces.

Is there less reason to marvel in them now
just because we have grown hardened
       and cynical?

Have we forgotten how to appreciate the world
            in wonder and praise?

The beauty of creation reveals the work of God,
                but at the same time,
like a mantle,
            it conceals him.

He wraps it around himself,
                yet remains above it.

You stretch out the heavens like a tent; you set
        the beams of your chamber upon the water.
You make the winds your messengers; you set
        the earth on its foundation.
You make the springs gush forth in the valleys,
        and they flow between the hills.
From your lofty abode you water the mountains;
        the earth is satisfied with the fruit of your
            your work.
You cause the grass to grow for cattle and plants
        for people to eat.
You make wine to gladden the human heart and
        oil to make the face to shine.
The trees of the Lord are watered abundantly;
        in them the birds build their nests.
The high mountains are for the wild goats; the
        rocks are a refuge.
You made the moon to mark the seasons; the
    sun knows its time for setting.
You make the darkness and the light.

The young lions roar for their prey, seeking
their food from God.
People go out to do their work and they labor
until the evening.
The sun rises and the sun withdraws.

O Lord, how manifold are your works; in
wisdom you made them all.
To you they look to give them their food in
due season.
When you give it, they gather it.
When you open your hands, they are filled
with good things.
When you hide your face, they are dismayed.
When you take their breath, they die and
return to dust.

cf. Psalm 104:2-29

Can we see in the words
of the psalm of praise
such a spirit of thanksgiving and wonder
in all that God has done?

God places all manner of beautiful things
and graces
and gifts
along our path.

He calls us up
from within the hardness of our hearts,
into the oases,
the Edens
which are all around us.

28

And if we take the time to ask,
      "Why, O why?"
our heart will be freed by grace
to offer to God
        its own response to that question
in praise and thanksgiving.

As the mind says,
      "Why, O why?"
  the heart says
      "My, O my!"

The heart begins to perceive
      all the created order around it
          as a benediction.
The heart begins to interpret it
     as a grace,
     as a gift
from the hand of God.

This must be our basic and spontaneous response
     to life.

It is only when we have such an attitude
that we will be able
to wrestle with the many other questions,
      the many other kinds of "Why?"
that frequently preoccupy us.

The very wonder of our being,
the beauty of the earth
and all that is in it
should forever induce us
to make of our lives
a constant hymn of praise,
a constant song of thanksgiving.

"Bless the Lord, O my soul."

II

The Impulse for Gratitude

The Liturgy of the Church proclaims the fact
that we were made
to praise and to thank God.

Many Christians hear such expressions
              and smile
at how "quaint" that sounds.
We were made,
they imagine,
          for very serious work,
              very tedious activity.

Praising and thanking God,
they think,
is a pastime
      for the "leisure class" of Religious.

If there *is* a God,
          they reason somewhat rightly,
he does not require our praise
                    or thanksgiving.
He is satisfied in himself
and doesn't need to be flattered.

When many Christians consider
the praise and thanksgiving
that are being offered up
              in the Church's age-old rites,
they think:

"How primitive of the Ancients
to keep heaping up glory onto God
who,
if he really is supreme,
        must be indifferent and unmoved."
It probably seems to them
to be some arcane manner
            of trying to manipulate him.

You know how it is,
                    humanly speaking.
So many people praise and compliment
the one
over whom they hope to gain an advantage.

With this kind of sentiment in the Church,
the whole project of praise and thanksgiving
receives progressively
            less and less emphasis.
People start thinking
            that there are much more important things
about which they need to occupy themselves.

If they have time at the end of the day for prayer,
                or at the end of the week
                        for communal worship;
if they have time at the end of the year
                        for adoration at the manger,
or, as it is becoming for many,
                    at the end of their life
                                for anointing,
then maybe they will think about acknowledging God.

34

So today we need to declare it again:
the project of praise and thanksgiving
    is *not* secondary.
It is not a pastime,
                or an option.
It is essential.

Certainly God has no need of our praise.

The people of God who offer worship and praise
are not foolishly and primitively imagining
                that they can flatter a deity
into submission.

The Celebrant of the liturgy intones:
        "You have no need of our thanks, yet our
        desire to thank you is itself your gift."

It is for *us*
                that worship and thanks
are offered to God--
        for our well-being and redemption,
        for our welfare and peace.

Thanksgiving and praise
are the surest means of orienting the heart
toward the direction of the life-giving One
                who is the object
of that thanksgiving
    and praise.

If you have ever been in the presence
                        of someone whom you admire,
then so long as you allowed yourself
            to be admiring,
you felt the purity of our original innocence;
you felt the heart turning outward,
blossoming in the presence
            of the light of another,
basking in the warmth
and the goodness of the other.

Admiration is unconsciously filled with praise.

It's almost embarrassing
    how much we want to thank
                    and to praise an admirable soul;
we take pleasure in doing so.

But in our society and in our culture,
we have grown careful
not to be too effusive in our declarations
                when we admire someone.
We are free to vent our cynicism,
but, alas,
not our impulse to admire.

But there are sunnier peoples;
    there are other cultures
in which,
            when the heart is filled,
it declares itself;
it spills over.

It doesn't consider so much
            the cost of embarrassment
as it does the pleasure
to honestly make itself known.

For never is the intention of the heart better known
than when it overflows
            with thanksgiving and praise.
Then the water courses are clear,
                        unobstructed,
and what pours out of the heart finds its object.
The heart is satisfied for a moment
that it has exercised itself
            with vitality.

Praise and thanksgiving
are the means
            by which the heart comes to life,
    the means
            by which it is directed towards the object
            which can fulfill,
                    and satisfy,
                    and restore,
                    and heal it.

The ultimate object of our heart's desire
            is God.

The admiration of God
is the greatest exercise
            of day-to-day love
and worship.

Therefore,
our praise and gratitude to God
is the surest way
to orient ourselves
            outside the abyss of darkness
                        which we have become,
and to open ourselves
            to the brightness of divine light.
Even from our darkness
            all the more
            do we admire the light
                        and desire it
for ourselves.

Praise and thanksgiving are the essence
                        of the Eucharistic life,
for "eucharist" surely means
            not just the table of sacrifice;
it also describes
            the intentionality,
            the orientation of the soul
to gratitude.

All of the great saints
            of the Church's mystical life
have said
      that praise is the highest form of prayer.

Praise is the acknowledgement
      of who God is
and what God is.

Thanksgiving is its twin.

Thanksgiving is the acknowledgment
of what God does.

Praise and thanksgiving
are really inseparable,
          in fact.
Although we can distinguish them in our mind,
the difference between who God is
                    and what God does
we can separate
          only abstractly.

He *is* the Source of all Goodness;
what he *does* is the Pure Act of Goodness.

The actuality
          of who God is and what God does
forms a seamless unity
                    of our experience of God
because even when we experience who he is,
it is a revelation
          of what he is doing,
          and how he makes himself known to us.

So when we offer God praise
          we are already thanking him;
     when we thank him,
          we are already praising him.

Thanksgiving and praise
          are the prayer life of the soul
          and the prayer life of the Church.

39

They are the acknowledgement
 of the presence
 and the activity of God.

Praise and thanksgiving
 are what Jesus exemplified
 in his earthly life
at every turn.

On one occasion in his public life,
 apparently in the midst of other activities,
Christ looked up to heaven
and blurted out before his apostles
these words:

> *"Blessed are you, Lord God, for what you have hidden
> from the learned and the clever, you have revealed to
> the merest children. Father, it is true. You have gra-
> ciously willed it so."*

 cf. Matthew 11:25-26

The disciples looked at each other
 as Jesus prayed
and nodded their heads.
They had now grown accustomed
 to these spontaneous outbursts
of thanksgiving.

Jesus had a manner of gratitude
 which punctuated his daily life.

40

So frequently was he filled
            with the admiration of his Father
that it overflowed from him in prayer.
He spoke his gratitude;
he radiated it.

When he dined,
        in particular,
he was frequently overwhelmed with gratitude,
because reclining at table
conjoined all of the finest gifts
                and greatest works of God.
It was there
that the best of nature and creation
was presented
            as food and drink.

Around the table--
especially the banquet table
            of which he spoke so often--
were the highest forms
            of human culture and art:
    the craft of the furniture,
    the design in the tapestries,
    the patterns in the carpet,
    the play of light through the windows.

Reclining at table provided the best
that love could give:
        social discourse,
        the blessing of convivial conversation
    and the marvelous interchange
of all of the elements of gracious hospitality.

When Jesus reclined at table,
he was taking into himself
the best of nature and creation
                in the exchange of food.

He was also taking into himself
the companionship
                of all those around him.

Jesus was overwhelmed with thanksgiving,
                        emotionally and spiritually,
just as we are often so filled
        at a meal among friends.

Why do people carry on the most important works
                    of social discourse at table:
celebrating birthdays and anniversaries,
deepening relationships,
proposing marriage,
signing contracts,
gathering in-laws into the family?

Why do people place so much of a burden on a meal?

Because silently,
            unconsciously,
there is in a meal
            the exchange of life to life
                        and heart to heart.
as food which is possessed by all
                    is distributed to each.

Those who host it
give themselves away
          by the very food they have provided.
Life is co-mingled,
          conjoined
     and shared.

The meal was for Jesus
                    the opportunity
to offer all of these blessings to God
in gratitude.

Christ often likened the kingdom of God
               to a meal,
               a party,
               a banquet,
               a wedding feast,
and he often spoke his most winning words
to his disciples
at table.

Perhaps the most beautiful short story
                    in all of literature,
was spoken by Jesus
                    as he reclined at table.

He was enjoying a festive meal
with people who had accustomed themselves
                    to being left outside:
tax collectors,
sinners.

Mary of Magdala was probably there,
          with several other women
                    who were like her.

The Pharisees and Scribes
were murmuring at the door:

> *"This man welcomes sinners and eats with them."*
>   Luke 15:2

In response
Jesus told the story of the Prodigal Son
                    which is really a parable
of a heart filled with gratitude.

When we read this parable,
it can fill our hearts as well;
          because it is so filling,
                    and nourishing.
It's almost like a wedding feast.

In Biblical language,
the prayer at a meal was called "breaking bread"
because the prayer was typically prayed
          after the first act of common dining
was offered,
that is,
          when the bread was broken.

The expression "breaking bread"
has become a euphemism
                    for the whole process of dining
and the whole process of praying.

44

"Breaking bread"
       means to pray thanksgiving--
              to pour out a heart of praise
and thanksgiving
at a meal.

Apparently
       the manner by which Jesus broke bread,
       the manner by which he prayed,
       the manner by which he thanked God
was distinctive.

These joyous outbursts,
these intense feelings of mutuality with his friends,
these spontaneous aspirations for his Father,
these heart-felt blessings
were his signature.

Even on the road to Emmaus
his disciples did not recognize him
              when he explained the Scriptures,
"though their hearts were burning within them."

They did not recognize him by the companionship
that he offered,
though they walked on the road with him
              so many miles.

They did not recognize him face to face
                            in their home
until he broke bread with them
at a meal.

No one was so filled with thanksgiving
             as was Jesus.
No one else
          had such a signature of praise.

It was unmistakable.

The two disciples recognized him by his prayer,
                              by his thanksgiving.
And when that prayer was finished,
he vanished
because *that* was how they were to remember him:
          filled with thanksgiving
                    and praise.

That is how we, too, must remember him.

When he said, *"Do this in memory of me,"*
he was giving us a vocation--
                    a call
to accomplish in our own lives
a similar work of thanksgiving
                    and praise.

We will never really be happy
until we have turned to God
             in such a manner as this.

How do we look at the world when we look at it?

If we live in the perception
                    of a secular society,
we look out over our world every morning
and we see certain opportunities
                          to be exploited,
            certain problems to be solved,
            certain obstacles to be overcome.

We also see a great deal of indifferent matter
which is neither obstacle nor opportunity for us:
gray matter
that fades out of our interest.

Such is the perception of a secular world.
How drab and tedious!

What is the perception of the Church
                    and of a spiritual mind?

What is the perception of a believer?

Waking up in the morning
we should be overcome with gratitude
                    that we are alive.
As we open our eyes,
        life pours in;
        sensation is revitalized.
We are overwhelmed
            with the grace and the glory
of the senses.

Life is impossibly rich and diverse,
        unimaginably superabundant.
It gives us a clue
about the generosity of God.

Praise and thanksgiving should well up within us
        spontaneously.

It did once
        when we were very young.

Every moment that we were awake
was filled with gratitude,
                wonder
        and praise.

There still is in us that opportunity, that possibility.

If there were not such a foundation in us,
I think that we would die.

The spark of life
provides the possibility of gratitude,
        the possibility of turning outward
to the giver of gifts
in admiration and thanksgiving.

Unbelievably
we find ourselves every day
                here
in this world.
We don't deserve to be here.
We didn't do anything
                        to merit
                    or to cause it.

We are simply here again,
                    present again
to the world.

How marvelous!
How overwhelming!
How unaccountable!

Everything that we experience
is an undeserved blessing for us
                just because we experience it,
                just because we have been placed
        in the world
        in such a time
and in such a way
as to encounter it.

The Eucharistic life
evokes a different perception
                    than the groaning
                    and the complaining
of life
in this world.

And so we must ask ourselves:
                what is *our* perception;
                what perception do we cultivate,
                                and foster?
What perception do we trust,
                and exercise?

We are followers of Christ,
and he has shared with us
the capacity
                to see our lives
as blessing.

It was so with us,
                originally,
but we have lost that perspective.

He gives us anew,
                unreservedly,
the grace to find it again,
in him.

We can live in his presence
                and see what he sees.

Most especially
we can live in the fellowship
                that he enjoys
by living our lives
                in his bond
with the Father.

For the longest time I assumed
          that the "our" in the Our Father
meant "your Father and mine."

But now I understand
          that when we pray "our Father,"
we mean "his Father and ours."

You and I
are praying in conjunction with Christ.

He has shared the bond of his sonship with us,
and only in this sharing
are we able to become God's children.

That bond,
          as the Easter Liturgy proclaims,
restores for us a lost innocence;
it brings mourners joy
and levels earthly pride.

That bond
gives us the perception
                    of blessing and gratitude
at every turn.

What did Jesus say to Mary Magdalene at the tomb
on Easter morning?

> *"Go to my brothers and tell them 'I am ascending
> to my Father and to your Father, to my God and
> to your God!'"*   John 20:17

The foundation of the Lord's Prayer
is the "our"
       that Jesus revealed to Mary Magdalene
in the garden.

And that is the foundation of our gratitude--
      that we should be so conjoined
            in a bond with God
      that we can speak through the lips of Christ:
       "through him and with him and in him."

With him
we can enjoy a fellowship
that is utterly undeserved
      and unimaginable.
And in that fellowship
everything
      is blessing and gift.

Our hearts turn outward in praise
and thanksgiving.

What we need
is a gentle openness
      to grow in thanksgiving--
not because God needs it,
but because he offers it to us
as a gift.

We profoundly need
to be filled with gratitude
      in order to enjoy our fellowship with Christ
and with one another.

III

The Garden of Delight

W e are told in Chapter 2 of Genesis that:

The Lord God formed man out of the clay of the ground and blew into his nostrils the breath of life, and so man became a living being.
Genesis 2:7

First, I note to you
        that the one that God created in the Garden,
            the one that he created out of the earth
                    from clay
was not yet named
in this verse of Genesis.

The word for "taken from the earth,"
        or "taken from the soil--
                groundling"
in Hebrew is "*Adama.*"

And so the creature who was first created by God
is identified
        not yet by a personal name,
        but by his origin:
"taken from the earth: Adama."

You will remember
that Moses was given his name
        because "he was taken from the water."
Adama was given his name
because he was taken from the earth.

Adama was not yet a human being
                    in the way we are.

He could not be, for he was alone.

What is a human being
alone,
        without mother or father,
        without brother or sister,
        without spouse or child?

Such a being we do not know.

Nor would we recognize Adama--
                    the one made from the earth--
                    as one quite like ourselves.

We know he is not one like ourselves
because he was possessed
                    in some mysterious way,
"physically,"
of parts unlike our own.

He had
what may symbolically be described
                    as "an extra rib"
which would later be removed from him.

Surely this passage is not to be taken literally;
men and women have the same number of ribs.

Surely the author of Sacred Scripture
did not intend to record an anatomical description
            of the creative processes of God!

It's rather amazing
            that in the earliest books of anatomy,
biologists numbered the ribs of men and women
differently,
presuming that men had one less rib
            than women
because God took one out of Adama
and formed it into Eve!

But something was taken from the groundling;
      something was removed which he was now lacking,
and someone else had it!

Indeed,
the loss of this "rib" so altered Adama
            that at the moment of his waking
                        after it was taken from him
he was at last himself,
as new
as the creature that was presented to him.

And in that moment
            when Adama became aware of his lack,
he became a searcher;
he became a seeker
            to find himself.

At the same time,
he became a seeker to find the other one:
the one
who had part of himself

within her.

He became a seeker
          for the one who would complete him,
               the one who would round out
what was missing in himself.

In that act,
          at that moment,
we can recognize him.

He became one just like us.

In that moment,
          Adama became a man,
          and Eve became a woman.

And so we can easily reconcile this story of creation
with the account of the first chapter of Genesis
when God said:

> *"Let us make man in our own image, after our own*
> *likeness." So God created man in his image; in the*
> *divine image he created them; male and female he*
> *created them.*   Genesis 1:26-27

We know that there is in God
          in the ageless bond of the Trinity,
   mutuality and reciprocity,
a communality of heart to heart,
a communion of love.

No wonder then
that when God created us
        "in the divine image and likeness,"
he created us
            male and female.
No wonder then
that he created us
        with a conspicuous lack
        and a significant need--
an incompleteness.

Searchers and seekers we will always be
            to find that which was lost,
                that which was removed.
Searchers and seekers we will always be
            to delight in whatever can be given us
to lead us back toward wholeness.

In our Church,
marriage is a sacrament.
It is not just a necessary evil
            to deal with concupiscence.
It is not just a necessary means
            to procreate the race.
It is not some faint avocation,
            a distraction
from our more essential spiritual pursuits.

Marriage is the sacrament given to us by Christ
            which empowers men and women
to become mutual ministers
of the grace of God
to one another.

What married couples discover
is
that they are not yet complete
            in their mutuality with one another.
They discover
that their mutuality
            for each other
    and with each other
is itself
hearkening to the communality in God,
to the bond
            of the Father and the Son.

In their love for each other,
            they discover a deeper yearning,
                        a hunger and thirst.
As Christians,
they express their aspirations
            through common prayer,
            through coming together
                        to the table of the Lord.

They share an openness to the presence
            of the Father and the Son and the Holy Spirit
in the intimacy of their lives.

We are told in the Book of Genesis
that Adama,
the groundling,
was placed in the Garden
            that God had planted.
It was filled with trees
            that were delightful to look at
and good for food.

Adama was given a project
           to name every creature
                      that God presented to him,
and he delighted in naming them.

Then Eve was created and given to Adam,
                              now a man,
and they found delight in each other,
           the delight of mutuality--
social delight.

They moved from delight in sight
           to delight in taste
           to delight in speech
           to delight in communality
and love with each other.

They were progressing up a ladder
           step-by-step
                toward delighting in God,
                toward oneness
with God.

Notice
that when they were given mutuality
                and love for each other,
they were not deprived
           of the Garden and the animals
                that Adam had formerly named.
These things were not like rungs
           that were discarded
once they had climbed above them.

They now had each other
and they continued to enjoy the Garden.

And if they had persevered
            in their journey toward God,
they would have continued to have each other,
            with all other things subsumed
into the love of God.

The vocation of gratitude
is one of an infinite ability
            to receive generously,
            to receive continually more and more--
not losing what was given formerly,
but raising it up
            in every further act of reciprocity
with greater thanksgiving.

Adam and Eve discovered
that in gratitude
            there is a certain connaturality,
that is to say,
what is given
corresponds
            to something that is already in us.

When you hear a symphony
and the music is lovely to you,
how do you know
            that it is lovely?

A nonsensical question, you might say.

You know that immediately,
but how?--
except that there is already in you
the capacity to recognize beforehand,
            to understand in advance
                        what would be lovely
                        and what would attract.
There is already in you
the prefiguring of the beauty
            to which you are later drawn.

There is a connaturality
            when we are grateful,
            when we are thankful.

We find in our experience,
            in our social discourse with each other,
that there is already within us
something
            which corresponds to it.

It is a subtle thing.

That which we find wonderful,
                        attractive
                        and beautiful
is different from ourselves.

63

On the one hand we lack it.

On the other hand
it is also similar;
it resembles something within us.

It resembles the niche of that lack
                    that is within us--
the empty space
of that "missing rib."

Sometimes we meet people
toward whom we gravitate immediately.
We are interested in them;
we want to get to know them.

Why does this happen?

There must be an empty niche in us
                which corresponds to them.
That space
has the shape of their presence
and we are attracted to them.

In every act of gratitude
        there is gratitude
for that which is new
yet that which is the same;
for that which is different from us,
yet that which is similar to us.

This kind of delight
            is what Christ Jesus wishes to restore in us:
 this kind of ability
            to recognize with joy
                        that which is different
            and that which is similar,
and to see in them
a God who is crafting all things
            for our well-being
            and our happiness.

None of the animals in the Garden
                        were a suitable partner for Adama.
because there was no interplay
                        of that which was lacking
            and that which was present.

Something had to be taken from him;
something had to be missing.
Something else had to fill that space--
something that would correspond
                        to his need.

Then the interplay would become active,
                                    dynamic
                        and filled with energy.
Then the searching and the seeking,
                        the yearning
                        and the desire
would stab the heart.

Then mutuality would really become possible.

In the Slavic languages,
the word for "gender" or "sex"
                    is the word "half."
The implication is
        that one gender is half of the other,
and that to be engendered as male or female
is to be approximately
half
of what God intends us to be.

The trouble in our society today
                and in our Church today
is that many people
do not have a great deal of understanding
                    about these matters.
They are either tempted to think
that marriage is not holy at all,
or, that
        if it is a sacrament,
then everyone must participate
and there should never be celibacy in the Church.

The mutual love of God
can be revealed in married love
but it can also be revealed in the celibacy
                    of the Church's religious life--
and the chastity of a single life.

What was "not good" before the time of Christ
became, after the mission of Jesus,
a great good for some
and a great blessing for many.

The chaste and celibate priest,
the chaste and celibate religious,
the chaste and celibate single person of faith
reveal in their bodies
the sign
that Christ Jesus is present to us
        so intimately,
        in so many mysterious ways,
that even the primal and primary way to God,
that of nuptial love,
is already enfolded
in the grace of sacramental signs
        and communal fellowship.

Human marriage has not been superseded,
but the mysterious foundations of its eternal value
have been revealed
        in the filial love
           of the Father and the Son
and the fraternal love of Christ
        and his disciples.

The life of chastity and celibacy
and the mutual life of husband and wife
are parallel to each other
and mutually enrich each other.

They are both signs
of how we should delight in the gifts of God:
conjoined in marriage
or united with Christ,
      alone,
in faith.

Both of these vocations
are lived fully in our Church;
both
are Eucharistic lives
of praise and thanksgiving.

This thanksgiving
which was already anticipated
            in the Garden of Eden
has as its primary goal
our union with God.

When the serpent came into the Garden,
the gratitude of Adam and Eve was put to the test.

The serpent insisted
that God was withholding gifts
which were rightfully theirs.
He was keeping them for himself,
even fearful
            that if they ate of the fruit
                        of the tree of knowledge
they would become like unto him.

And so the hearts that had been filled
            with delight,
            with thanksgiving and gratitude
                        for all that they enjoyed
became preoccupied
with that which had not yet been given
with that which they came to feel
            was being withheld.

Their delight and gratitude hardened
                    into impatience
and distrust.

They reached for these gifts
            before they were ready
            before their love had matured,
            before their walk with God
                        had much advanced.
They became, first, covetous
            and then, disobedient.

We, too, can become infected
            by the poison of covetousness.
We, too, can become so preoccupied
                        observing what others have
that we are filled with resentment
for what we have not.

We can become so busy
concerning ourselves with the blessings of others:
                        their social skills
                        their popularity,
                        their education,
                        their intelligence,
                        their wealth,
                        their looks,
                        their health,
                        their spouse,
                        their family and friends,
that our delight in the gifts of God
which we now enjoy
            is dissipated,
and our gratitude is dissolved.

One of the greatest dangers of covetousness
is the failure to recognize
                    what God has given us,
to ignore the blessings
                    which are already ours.

We neglect to count the blessings,
                    and the graces
                    which are poured out all around us,
and instead,
we bemoan those which are still lacking,
                    still missing,
                    still wanting.
We do so with accusation
            and recrimination.

The project of thanksgiving is forgotten.

We become interiorly impoverished
            by continually making comparisons
to what others have.

To live a Eucharistic life,
we must, first, be grateful for what we have
and then,
we must be grateful even for what we lack,
for what we lack
            gives us the capacity
                    to be open to receive,
                    to be available
for blessings.

70

This is what God teaches
    in the creation of Eve in the Garden.

How did Adam react when he first saw her?
Was he angry and resentful
        for being wounded,
        for feeling empty
and broken?

No.
Adam rose to the occasion and said:
    "This one, at last, is flesh of my flesh and bone
    of my bones!"   cf. Genesis 2:23

He found a greater satisfaction
        in having her
        in his incompleteness
than having been formerly complete
        in himself.
He found that being fulfilled
in her
was better
    than being unfulfilled
in himself alone.

"At last," he said,
as if being filled with continuous delight
        in the Garden of God
was somehow poverty
        compared to what he now had
in her presence.

In our society,
we are taught to be covetous
from our earliest years.

The TV reminds us
        of what others have
        that we have not;
the commercials remind us
                of the gifts
that they enjoy
and we do not.

And always being paraded before us
                for our torture and intimidation,
are people of higher classes
        and higher estates
                with material benefits
we can't even imagine.

And always
we are feeling poorer,
                weaker,
                helpless
        and threatened.

Covetousness is death to the soul
        and death to prayer
for it chokes the fountain of thanksgiving
                which ordinarily rises up within us
in gratitude to God.

Better than looking with envy or jealousy
                              at others
would be
to pause when we notice them
and say to God:

　　"Thank you for what they have that I have not.
　　Thank you for the gifts they have that I do not.
　　Thank you for the blessings they have
                                    that I have not."

We are taught,
                after all,
that in the Body of Christ
what one has,
        one has for all.

Whatever gifts of intelligence,
                or grace
                or beauty
that one has in the Body of Christ,
we all have,
        for all of us are conjoined
in his Body.

The celibate person is grateful
        for the married love others enjoy
as celibates share in their communion.

Celibate souls
offer praise and thanksgiving
        even for their "aloneness"
as a blessing from the Body of Christ.

And so we are rich
        in the riches of others
and rather than looking at them with envy,
                        poisoned for what we lack,
we can now look at them with blessing,
                        grateful for what they have.

For in the same moment
                        that we see what they have,
we can also begin to enjoy it ourselves
in the oneness of Christ.

Christ has restored to us
the life of gratitude and thanksgiving--
not so much through the Book of Nature
                as through the Book of his Word;
not so much through the fruit of the tree in the Garden
                as through his body
hanging upon the tree of the Cross.

Christ hung upon the Cross
                totally stripped of all things--
the poorest man of our race,
yet the richest in generosity.

Through his open side
poured out
                all the mercy of the heart of God,
which restored to us
                all that Adam and Eve had lost
through their disobedience.

From Adam's side
a "rib" was removed
                and Eve was brought forth.
From Christ's heart
                flowed out blood and water
and his Bride was espoused.

Christ came to give us life,
        a life of delight,
        a life of blessing.

In union with him
we can walk through the garden of this world
and grow in love
                toward union with God.

We can enjoy the Eucharistic banquet
he has prepared for us
                here and now
so that one day
we shall enjoy
that eternal banquet with him for ever
                in gratitude,
                        praise
                and thanksgiving.

IV

Externalizing Thanks

In Psalm 50, we hear a sentiment which is expressed
in a variety of ways in many Biblical passages.
The Psalmist says:

> *Hear, my people, and I will speak;*
> *Israel, I will testify against you;*
> > *God, your God am I.*
> *Not for your sacrifices do I rebuke you*
> > *for your holocausts are before me*
> > > *always.*
> *I take from your house no bullock;*
> > *no goats out of your fold.*
> *For mine are all the animals of the forests,*
> > *beasts by the thousands on my mountains.*
> *I know all the birds of the air,*
> > *and whatever stirs in the plain belongs*
> > > *to me.*
> *If I were hungry, I should not tell you,*
> > *for mine are the world and its fullness.*
> *Do I eat the flesh of strong bulls,*
> > *or is the blood of goats my drink?*
> *Offer to God praise as your sacrifice*
> > *and fulfill your vows to the Most High;*
> *Then call upon me in time of distress;*
> > *I will rescue you, and you shall glorify*
> > > *me. "*

Psalm 50:7-15

The Psalmist states something of the paradox
of the worship of the temple.

On the one hand,
God prescribed a ritual for Israel:
the offerings of lambs and sheep
and goats and oxen.

He ordered
the offerings of doves;
the offerings of the first fruits
        of wheat,
           grain,
           oil
and wine.

God prescribed it,
so the children of Israel were called to obey.
And then,
almost as if to trip them up,
he said:
        "I'm not hungry.
         These things you cannot give me;
         I own them already."

The people of Israel
were always wrestling with this paradox
of a God
who commanded them to give him all things
                in thanksgiving
and then who said:

        "What are you trying to do--manipulate me?"

Many relationships may seem like that.

I know people
who require from those they love
          gifts
        and signs
        and tokens.

And then in the very midst of getting gifts
                              and signs
                              and tokens,
they become indignant,
thinking that the person they love
is trying to coerce them.

It almost seems
that God was offering such a cross-signal
                    to the children of Israel.

But that was not the case.

God was not giving the cross-signal;
                    Israel was.
For Israel had forgotten
                    that a thanksgiving offering
is just that:
an expression of thanksgiving.

But she sometimes thought
                    that by making such an offering
she was entitled to divine favors.

Sometimes Israel thought
that she could control the unfolding Providence of God
                              by following exactly
the prescriptions of worship
which were given in the Law.

And just as soon as Israel was persuaded
that she was offering to God
                  that which he had not,
so that he would do what she intended,
God said:
                    "Stop!
            I'm not hungry anymore.
            I don't want any more gifts!"

Maybe you have been in that same position.

When someone has something you would like to have
and he is offering it to you,
and everything inside you instinctively says:
            "Don't take it; it isn't a gift.
            There are so many strings attached
            that you are liable to trip in a moment.
            It's not worth it.
            Let it go."

Follow your instincts.
Almost universally
they are right in such matters as this.

If there's a gift
you absolutely do not want to receive,
refuse it.

God did.

He would not accept the gifts of the Israelites
because the people who were offering them
were not giving them to him in gratitude.

They were not offering them in love,
and it wasn't delight
        that animated them.
They had forgotten
        that all the gifts of the field
were God's to begin with.

The dandelions we offered to our mother as children
were from the lawn
        that our parents already owned.

We are only offering to God what he already has.

A certain humility
is incumbent upon
        even our greatest acts of giving.
What can we give to God
that he does not already own?

Maybe there *is* one thing
that God has determined not to have,
        not to own--
one thing that God has permitted
not to count among his deeds of possession:
        our heart
        and its gratitude.

He leaves it up to us.

After having created us,
after having a moral right to possess us,
he surrenders his divine prerogative
                              of ownership
and leaves it to us to decide
              what we will give
and even *whether* we will give.

> *"Offer me a sacrifice of thanksgiving."*

This is what God desires.

If God could be spoken of
              as being hungry or thirsty,
it would be the self-offering
              of our gratitude and praise
that he would desire.

Jesus, in his agony on the Cross
refused the vinegar mixed with wine
which was held up on a sponge
to his lips.

He refused it
even though he had said,

> *"I thirst,"*

leaving us with the paradox
                    of a thirsting Savior
who would not drink
what people ordinarily drank
in their thirst.

Perhaps he was thirsting for our self-donation,
        thirsting for the offering of our lives,
    our gratitude,
and our surrender to God.

This sacrifice of thanksgiving
is such an antidote
to the kind of life we might otherwise live.

Our business in life
must become more and more
            an offering to God
day-to-day
and hour-to-hour
in praise and thanksgiving.

If we are not pouring ourselves out
to God
        in such a fashion as this,
we are liable to be drinking in
the toxins of our own complaining
            and lamenting,
day-by-day
and hour-by-hour.

If we are not centered on the heart of Christ
        and centered on the mystery
            of God's outpouring love,
if he is not the one who engages us,
then we are going to be absorbed
in ourselves.

This religion of self-absorption
is the pervasive idolatry
                    of our age.
It is the cult of the narcissist,
      the sect
which has seduced our present generation.

There are many in the Church,
who are worshiping at the altar
                    of self-absorption
as much as are the pagans and agnostics
                    the doubters and the scoffers.

In ancient Israel,
there were Levites in the temple
who
      on their "days off"
would go to the high places
and offer up idolatrous sacrifices
                    to Moloch and pagan deities,
hedging their bets,
in case there was more than one god.

Like the Levites,
there are many Christians
      and even Catholics
who worship at the altar of the self
and spend their days lamenting every slight,
                    complaining of every inconvenience
                    and murmuring against every restraint,
instead of offering to God
                    their sacrifice of praise.

This self-absorbed,
this egocentric kind of existence,
        the mantra of "me, me, me"
is the death of prayer
which would otherwise say to God,
"you, you, you!"

Thanksgiving is filled
with an acknowledgment of the Other,
        the one who loves us,
        the one who humbled himself
                to become a "thou" for us;
someone we can call to
        by the personal pronoun "you,"
someone we can even address
        by the personal possessive pronoun,
"*my* God."

The personal possessive pronoun "my"
is the operative word of prayer--
the prayer of investment,
        outpouring,
        surrender,
and acceptance.

God was always "my God" to Jesus,
and Jesus was always in dialogue
        with such an intimate God as this.
Even in the dereliction of his abandonment
                on the Cross,
he still cried out,
"my God!"

This is the dialogue
that God wishes to engage in with us
and the provisioning of this dialogue
is like a banquet.
God nourishes us with food and drink,
                    with bread and wine.

We are fed in this dialogue;
it is not just an abstract act
                    of the mind and will.

God provisions us,
for he wishes above all things
that we will continue in this dialogue
with him.

And so the soul says:

> *You spread a table before me*
> *You anoint my head with oil;*
>   *my cup overflows.*
> *Only goodness and kindness follow me*
>   *all the days of my life;*
> *And I shall dwell in the house*
>   *of the Lord*
>   *for years to come.*

Psalm 23:5-6

The Psalmist
is the voice of the human soul
who sees herself living in God's own house,
                    seated at God's own table,
offering up the sacrifice of the food
            which God has presented--
offering it back to God
with gratitude.

The Lord is my life's refuge;
of whom should I be afraid?
My foes and my enemies
themselves stumble and fall.
One thing I ask of the Lord,
this I seek:
To dwell in the house of the Lord
all the days of my life,
That I may gaze on the loveliness
of the Lord
and contemplate his temple.
For he will hide me in his abode
in the day of trouble;
He will conceal me in the shelter
of his tent,
he will set me high upon a rock.
Even now my head is held high
above my enemies on every side.
And I will offer in his tent
sacrifices with shouts of gladness;
I will sing and chant praise to
the Lord.

Psalm 27:1,3,4-6

Even though her foes are all around,
the soul throws back her head and laughs
because God is nearer than her foes,
closer than her enemies,
more intimate than her difficulties,
more proximate than her suffering.

God should be nearer to us
than our own pain
our own grief,
our own doubt.

89

Gratitude in the midst of all our adversities
is the sign of sanctity.

But most of the time,
alas,
we are more aware of all our foes
        than of the table set before us.

We are more aware of all our troubles,
                        and our problems,
the people who are our burdens,
the difficult ones
who hover around us like a cloud.

We often wonder:

        "Is God somewhere out there behind them,
        or beyond them?
        Can we find him in spite of them--
        all of these terrible people
        and events
        and difficulties
        and burdens
        which obscure our sight?"

But God is nearer to us,
                dearer for us
than all of these other distractions
                and diversions.

It is our responsibility to ourselves
            to be honest;
Simply *being* is a gift beyond measure.
It is our responsibility to God
            to be true.

All the blessings around us are gifts beyond number.

It remains for us
to offer up to him
            our prayers of thanksgiving;
to break out of the mantra
            of "me, me, me,"
and to break into the prayer
of "you, you, you."

This is to externalize,
            to make outward
that deepest desire of our inmost heart--
that deepest desire,
which
for great periods of time in our life
we are not in contact with.

We are restless and anxious,
not only because God seems to be indifferent,
      but because we have no access
                        to that inner chamber
where the deepest desire of our heart abides.

We are running busily to and fro
                  over the surface of our lives,
trying to do damage control with our problems,
trying to manage as best we can.

We do not release from within
                    that which would serve us best:
the offering of gratitude to God--
that outflow
                    of the inward part of our heart of hearts
which would wash back into us
a sense of the continuous favors and blessings
we receive from God.

We are orphaned from God
              because we are estranged from ourselves.

St. Augustine said:

          "God, it was not you who was far from me,
                    but it was I who was far from you.
          You were with me, but I was not with you."

Can it be
that just like Augustine,
we are also so fragmented,
              so broken,
              so bifurcated
that we are not even in touch
                    with our strongest and deepest longing,
                         our most interior dispositions
of love and gratitude?

We have every evidence in our daily lives
to believe
              that we really are
so fragmented and broken.

How many acts of the will
have we been able to perform
            flawlessly?

We wish to do good,
            but we fail to do it.
We wish to avoid evil,
            but we fail to avoid it.
We wish to go on a diet;
we wish to quit smoking;
we wish to stop gossiping,
            to stop wallowing in self-pity
but on and on we go,
doing the same things.

We give every evidence
that we are not at all in charge of our will,
nor of the deepest affects
                    which empower it.
We do not even know who we are
            or what lies deepest within us.

So it ought not to surprise us
that we have not always offered to God
the deepest prayer
            that wishes to rise up
from within.

Jesus said in the Gospel:

> *"The one who loves his life loses it, while the one who
> hates his life in this world will preserve it for life
> eternal."*   cf. John 12:25

We must ponder this observation of Christ,
especially in our culture
        and in our day
in which self-discovery,
            self-actualization,
            self-realization
        and self-fulfillment
are such highly touted goals to attain.

Ours is not like the religions of the Orient
which suggest
that dispersing oneself into the lonely void
is the best way to lose oneself.

We belong to the religion of the Revelation of Christ
which proclaims
that if you lose yourself
            in the love of Christ and his Cross,
you will find yourself
in God.

It is not the mirror,
        not our friends,
    or not our foes
who reveal to us who we are.

It is not the psychiatrist,
        not the I.Q. test,
        not the S.A.T.,
        not the Enneagram,
        nor the Meyers-Briggs test
which reveal to us who we are.

Only Christ can reveal to us our true self.

If we were angels,
there would be no need
to externalize the interior of our heart.

Angels
as pure spirits
have no interior or exterior.
They are one and the same
in every aspect of their being.

The disposition of each angel
is immediately apparent to every other one,
unmediated by activities,
          by efforts,
          or by desires.
Their intentions don't have to be externalized.
What is in a spirit
          is obvious at once.

Such is the life of heaven.

But we are wrapped in flesh;
we are embodied creatures.
What is in our spirit,
what is in our heart
          is not so obvious all at once.
We must strive to make it so;
we must seek
to make it appear.

We have to learn the art,
to make plain
                   on our face
                   and on our lips
the *intentions* of our heart--
not just the interests
                   of the moment.

We must externalize
             the delight of our soul,
             the joy of our heart;
we must make our gratitude clear.

This is necessary in every genuine human relationship.

Although we are not angels,
we have an advantage over them
that God finds quite stirring,
                   and so enchanting in us,
that he has eternally desired it
from us.

When we strive to externalize
the love
and the gratitude
             that is within us,
we do more than just make visible
                   what is invisible.

96

By the very exercise
of making our love and gratitude external,
we actually enhance the love
            which had been interior.
It actually increases
the gratitude.

When there is someone we love,
we wish to procure for him special gifts.
So already in early summer
we begin to rack our mind:

"What would be the perfect gift for Christmas?"

July, August and September wear on.

We ask the friends and family of the one we love:
            "What ideas have you?"
We search for hints;
we consider his every interest,
                        seeking an answer.
What would be the best gift?

But in the end,
no matter what we give him
            as the external sign of our love,
no matter what gift we make
                        or purchase,
did not the exercise
        of trying to find the right gift
actually deepen our love?

If the person is clever at all,
will he not receive the gift--
                no matter what it is--
more for the effort,
more for what it signifies
than for what is actually presented?

When we make our gift external,
        if we do it with art,
        if we do it with desire,
we perfect love,
we perfect gratitude.

Angels can't do that,
                so God did not become an angel!

God became a human being
because there is something in the nature
                        of the way we love
which God finds fascinating
                desirable
                and holy--
that here is a creature who struggles and yearns
        to perfect love--
        to make it external
again and again.

There is no end to love's perfectibility
                in the ongoing exchange of gifts.

How well does Hallmark know this!

People who are stammering
                and stuttering
                and tongue-tied,
                        faltering of speech
                and afraid of emotion
flood into Hallmark shops
to seek one of their thousands of possible verses
which would best describe their feelings.

This is the frustration of being a human being,
yet this is the finest art
                of being human as well.

All of us are caught up
                in the giving and receiving
of gifts,
of how to make visible,
                        verbal
                and tangible
the desires,
the love
and the gratitude
of our heart.

Even God himself
is now implicated
                in the struggle and the art!

The struggle was his Cross;
the art was his Last Supper,
and he assists us
whether we are struggling
under our own inability to express ourselves,
or whether we are released
                    into the freedom
of pouring ourselves out
in love.

It is Christ who escorts us
            in the joy of the one
and the frustration of the other
so that our whole life
can be,
in union with him,
a continual act of sacramental intimacy,
of offering to God
                our praise
and thanksgiving.

V

Gratitude in Co-Suffering

We are afflicted in every way possible, but we are not crushed; full of doubts, we never despair. We are persecuted but never abandoned; we are struck down but never destroyed. Continually we carry about in our bodies the dying of Jesus, so that in our bodies the life of Jesus may also be revealed. While we live we are constantly being delivered to death for Jesus' sake, so that the life of Jesus may be revealed in our mortal flesh.

2 Corinthians 4:8-11

In this passage
St. Paul advises us
that we are afflicted
            in every possible way,
that we are carrying about
            in our bodies
every day
the death of the Lord.

He says
that we are filled with doubts,
            but we never despair;
we are persecuted,
but we never give up.

He says in another passage
that we can even rejoice
in our afflictions!

How is it
that St. Paul could bear up so well
        under the pressure
of so many problems?

How is it
that he could speak so nobly
        under the weight
of so much adversity?

St. Paul thought
that the trials he endured
fostered a kind of intimacy with God.

By sharing in the death of the Lord,
by carrying about the Cross of the Lord
                        in his own body,
St. Paul believed
that he was sharing in the love of the Lord
                in its greatest sign,
                        its most positive proof
and that there was in him
        not just suffering,
        but co-suffering,
and co-suffering
is the strongest form of love
and affirmation.

I always like to consider
that a couple celebrating their Golden Jubilee
will have spent fifty years in marital love,
                        in mutual sacrifice
and surrender
and tears.

Consequently,
they have a deeper love
          than they had on their honeymoon,
because they have co-suffered,
and suffering conjoined
is intimacy confirmed.

We are told by veterans
that the deepest friendships
          that human society can afford,
          that life can offer,
are the friendships formed in the boot camp,
     and friendships formed on the battlefield--
places where people become melded together
by shouldering together
the heavy yoke of suffering.

And so
it is precisely *because*
we are afflicted in every way possible
it is precisely *because* we are persecuted,
     precisely *because* we are rejected
               and our fortunes reversed
that St. Paul says
we are not crushed
and we do not despair.

Because in all of the sufferings we endure
Christ Jesus suffers
          within us.
We carry about in our bodies
the death of the Lord.

Our dying and his dying
are conjoined--
            as is our suffering
             with his suffering.
And all things considered,
his suffering is infinitely harsher
                    more excruciating,
a greater offering,
a more honest surrender
to the will of God.

Two Beatitudes present this paradox sharply:

> *"Blessed are those who mourn;*
> *Blessed are those who are persecuted because of me."*
>   Matthew 5:4,10

How wonderful then,
to conjoin our suffering
        to his.
Ours is a tentative and hesitant offering to God;
our suffering
which is only *reluctantly* endured
would surely be evaded
            if there were any way possible
for to us to do so.

How generous,
how overwhelmingly gracious of God
to accept our suffering
            in union with that of Christ
which was endured with a fullness of resolve
in obedience to God
for love for us.

Christ Jesus says,

"My yoke is easy and my burden light."

He thereby advises us
that our relationship to him
is a yoke
and a burden.

A yoke in and of itself
is not something
that we would ordinarily be willing to accept.

It is something
which links two beasts together
neck to neck
so that by being co-yoked,
they can accomplish a specific task.

But this yoke
to which we have been joined,
is easy
and its burden light
because Christ carries the greater load.
He does the greater work
            by far.
He not only carries the greater weight of the burden
beyond our strength,
but he even carries the burden of our very selves.

Christ accomplishes the redemption of our lives,
because he accepts the gesture of our suffering
in union with his.

Christ accepts the offering of our poor obedience
            in union with his perfect obedience
                    and his penitential suffering.
He accepts the humble prayer of our thanksgiving
            in union with his great Eucharist
and his total donation to the Father.

It is for this reason
that the mystical tradition of our Church
is filled with saints
            who have endured tremendous afflictions
and have done so
with remarkable cheerfulness
and joy.

When we hear the stories of these saints,
we marvel
that they have endured so much
                    so well
and have offered God
            praise and thanksgiving
even in the midst of their suffering.

When I was in Egypt,
I stayed in the desert monasteries--
those monasteries
which are the most rustic and primitive
of all Christendom.

They were built in the third and fourth centuries,
and are the same today
as when they were first constructed.

The life--
the regime,
the discipline,
the austerity of the monks--
is as stark and as astounding
to the Westerner today
as it was to our forebears
when these monasteries were first built.

I was staying in the desert monastery
named after its founder,
St. Samuel.

It's one of the most remote outposts
of the Sahara,
and,
unfortunately,
I was staying there in July
because I was unable to follow the schedule
that I had originally planned.

In this particular stretch of the Sahara Desert,
the temperature soars in July
to what we would consider to be ungodly heights.
And just then,
while I was there,
a heat wave struck this region
with hotter than normal temperatures.

Every thermometer I had
burst
at temperatures over 140°,
so I was most inconvenienced and discomforted
in the monastery
which did not have electricity,
or central air
nor, it seemed,
even air itself!

109

So, of course,
there were no fans.

The sun was beating down
so fiercely
on the adobe bricks of the monastery,
that by the end of the afternoon
it had baked them
through and through.

All night long
like a convection oven,
the buildings were baking on the interior,
and we could feel the heat
pouring out of the walls.

I became delirious,
fading in and out of consciousness
as we took turns
going to the vat of well water
and poured cup after cup of it
over our heads.

The Abbot of the monastery was concerned
that I would die in his house,
causing all the inconvenience
of the body of a foreigner
that would have to be removed.

He didn't want to be responsible
for my death,
so he suggested that I make a journey
outside of the walls of the monastery
up to the mountain
where the founder had lived in a cave
nine hundred years ago.

This is the mountain
where St. Samuel had prayed
and God blessed his holiness
with the foundation of a monastery
under his tutelage.

The mountain was several miles distant
from the monastery.

The Abbot arranged
that an elderly monk--
really,
quite old and gaunt,
more gristle and bone
than muscle and flesh--
would lead me to the cave
of the founder.

We left the monastery in late afternoon
when the sun was setting
behind the crest of a large dune,
creating a little ribbon of shade
across the desert floor
that we could walk on.

The temperature of the sand was unmeasurably hot.

We had to walk barefooted
because we were walking on holy ground
to the cave of the founder,
and I was disturbed to discover
that my footprints were red
with the blood of my feet
as we walked!

The old monk was walking relatively fast,
but had me trudging on
ahead of him.

Under my breath I was muttering,
and murmuring,
grumbling and complaining
"against God and against Moses"
that I had been led out to suffer
in this terrible place.

I could hear the elderly monk behind me
murmuring too.

At first I paid no attention
because I grimly believed
that I was simply being led out into the desert
to die
outside the monastery.

At one point the monk even threw a rock at me--
at least,
it *seemed* to be thrown at me,
although it went over my head.

When I asked him why he did it,
he went ahead and picked it up.

Under the rock was a crushed scorpion
which,
it occurred to me,
had been poised to sting.

The monk was well aware of me,
so I became progressively more and more
aware of him.

As I began to listen
to what he was murmuring,
I could tell that it was melodic.

He was actually singing!

He was singing a spontaneous song in Arabic,
as a child sings,
right off the top of his head!
He was offering to God
a song of praise!

In his prayer,
he was singing something like this:

> "O God, I thank you and I praise you for this beauti-
> ful day in which you smile upon us with the strength
> of the sun and the warmth of your heart, a furnace
> of love. I thank you for our founder who came to
> this barren wasteland to cultivate a garden of grati-
> tude and praise in this house of prayer, this holy
> place of refreshment in the wilderness."

He was singing a song
filled with praise and thanksgiving
for the wonder and the beauty
of the day I was accursing!
He was able to see an Eden
in the midst of this wretched desert!

When we came to the base of the mountain,
he ascended it effortlessly,
almost as if he floated up
step by step.

However,
with every step I took
my feet sank.
For every three steps I took,
I fell back two steps
into the sand.

The monk reached the top of the mountain--
an elderly man over eighty,
I would guess.

And I, in my relative youth,
had gotten nowhere.

And then only for reasons of pride
did I scale the hill,
not willing to endure the idea
that this old monk was able to climb a mountain
that I could not.

When I got to the top,
he led me to the mouth of the cave
of the founder.
I didn't see it at first
as the opening was just a little crevice
that we couldn't walk into.

We had to slide into the cave
on our knees and our bellies,
some twenty, thirty or forty feet
into the earth.

All along the passage
I could hear the monk singing behind me.

When we reached the interior,
the crawl space opened up into a chamber.

The old monk lit a small candle
and then began to sing his Church's songs
of thanksgiving and gratitude
that we had reached the holy place,
the cave of the founder.

After he had sung for what seemed an hour or so,
he asked me to sing.

I was hoarse;
I was dry.

Our water had long ago run out
as I had drunk it all
in the first half hour of our walk.

We were now miles away from the monastery,
so far as I knew,
without water,
bound to be dehydrated
in a cave in the middle of the earth.

The old monk said,

> "Won't you sing me a song of praise and thanks-
> giving to God?   Won't you sing a hymn to the
> Virgin Mary from your Church so that we can offer
> up our praise and gratitude together?"

I thought to myself,
it was better not to commit murder in this cave
before my own death there.

So I sang the Salve Regina
and several other Marian hymns
in which he really delighted.
He asked me to sing them
over and over again.

After awhile he disappeared
further into the cave,
and then emerged
with a great pitcher of water
which he poured all over me
and gave me to drink.

It was cool, clear, sweet water,
not like the water of the monastery
which was saline and stagnant,
pumped out of the desert floor.

Apparently,
the founder of the monastery,
a thousand years before,
had constructed a system of fine grooves
that once or twice during the year
when it rained,
every drop of water on the hills
would collect in a cistern
deep in the depths of the mountain,
and would be stored there.

So then I realized
that the Abbot had sent me to this cave
not so that I would die,
but that I would live.

He had provided for me the best water
there was to drink
for hundreds of miles around.

I also realized
that the temperature in the cave
was 50° cooler than the air outside--
a refreshing 80°,
and even cooler yet
as I climbed down deeper into the mountain.

So I lived several days
in the prayer of gratitude and thanksgiving
in the cave of the founder
until the dangerous heat wave passed.

There is a lesson for us
            in such a zeal
as these monks have for prayer.
They really do count every affliction
as an occasion of thanksgiving.

They have deeply assimilated the truth
that every sorrow,
    every pain,
    every inconvenience,
    every discomfort
is a sharing
in the death of the Lord Jesus.

They have tapped into the wellspring
                of that truth,
and they are always refreshed.

If you read the sayings
of the desert fathers and mothers
which were recorded
      in the third, fourth,
          and fifth centuries,
you will read sayings of men and women
who lived in the most terrible conditions
of austerity and deprivation.

Some of these sayings have been collected
under the broad title of
The Paradise of the Fathers,
because these desert dwellers
     who co-suffered,
     and were co-yoked
        in the love of Christ,
        in the sufferings of Christ
     and lived in the mystery of his heart,
        in the shadow of his Cross
considered themselves
to be in paradise.

These monks have so assimilated this lesson
that the only thing they wish to do
is to praise and to thank God.

This praise and thanksgiving
is the other-centeredness
        which must mark our spiritual life.
It must be our goal.

We must be willing
to accept the progressive sanctification
of being centered
        on the One who is Other--
                the One who loves us in his suffering,
                        who calls us to endure our suffering
not simply as a problem
but as a gift
so that we can offer God praise and thanksgiving
even
in our afflictions.

Christ Jesus in his life on earth
was totally Other-centered.

He was filled with the presence of God,
            his Father: "Abba,"
and because his Father was so central to him,
he continually drew upon his presence.

From him he drew power for our healing
and fortitude for his mission.

He was one with the Father
and the Father was one with him.

He lived out that bond
        from beginning to end--
        from the womb of the Virgin Mary
to the wood of the Cross.

In every circumstance,
he offered himself in thanksgiving
to the Father.

"This is my body,"
he said to the Father in silence
when he was conceived
        in the womb of the Virgin.

"This is my body,"
he said to the Father
when he was presented to God
by Simeon in the temple.

"This is my body,"
he said to the Father
when he was dedicated anew to God
in the temple at the age of twelve.

"This is my body,"
he said to the Father
when he was baptized by John
at the River Jordan.

"This is my body,"
he said at the Last Supper
--at last aloud--
        presenting himself to the Father
while at the same moment
        presenting himself to the apostles,
and to us.

Then on the Cross,
he again offered himself in his body
                    to his Father
and in the tomb,
     in death,
he likewise offered himself to the Father,
wrapped in linens,
          in darkness
              behind a stone:
"This is my body."

And when in that darkness
the Father spoke his name:
     "Beloved Son,"
just as he had spoken it before:
     once at his Baptism,
and again at his Transfiguration,
the Savior's eyes opened
in obedience.

Christ Jesus rose up
          responding in exultation:
*"Abba, Father, **this** is my body,"*
               risen!
               glorious!
               alive!

His life was always an offering
          to his Father
in the best of times
and in the worst of times.

As a husband and a wife
      offer their bodies,
        their troth,
        their fidelity,
        their obedience
in the best of times
and in the worst of times,
they make the offering through the gesture,
               the gift,
               the outward sign
of their bodies.

And in this,
do they not image
the Eucharistic work of Christ?

For a husband and a wife
to count every adversity somehow a blessing
        because they share it,
to count every suffering somehow a gift
        because conjoined in love,
they endure it together
because being yoked
      and shouldered together,
they experience something of the essential mystery
of the Sacrament of Marriage.

But even that mystery
lies within a deeper mystery
      of the yoke of Christ
and his obedience to the Father.

It lies within the mystery
of his other-centeredness,
his willingness to carry his life
from beginning to end
as a gift to another.

And by the offering of that gift
to God his Father,
he offers himself in obedience
to us.

Genesis describes the faith of Abraham
who endured the barrenness of Sarah
for so many years.

Genesis likewise recounts the faith of Abraham
who endured the greed of his nephew Lot
and offered his own body,
his own life,
to ransom him
and save him from his foes.

Abraham offered his life and his body
in gratitude and thanksgiving.
Sarah did the same.

In this offering of their bodies to God
out of those bodies,
old and withered,
God confirmed his Covenant
by their miraculous conception
and birth of a son.

Out of the body of Christ,
              broken and bruised,
              wounded and dying,
God made a Covenant with us
so that in every circumstance,
              good or ill,
we can receive all things in gratitude
                        and thanksgiving,
offering ourselves to God
in union with Christ.

Just as the old monk
led me to a cave of cool refreshment,
so will our oblation of praise and thanksgiving
lead us to the refreshment
              of divine consolation.

God knows how much of the desert heat
we can take;
he knows how far on the journey
we can go.

There will be for us
some colossal struggle to climb a mountain
        where every step forward
will seem to take us
              two steps backward.
But in the end,
our gaze will open up
              into a surprising inner chamber
where our holy Founder awaits us
to shower us
with his cool refreshments.

123

VI

Fiat and Magnificat

During the earliest years
        of the history of Israel,
after the Hebrews had settled in Palestine,
there was a time
        in which their religious fervor
had grown relatively faint.

According to the Book of Samuel,
prophecies were rare,
        and visions unheard of.
The people of Israel
were less and less frequenting their "temple"
--actually the tent
        in which the Ark of God was kept
since the days of the Exodus.

The devotion of the people had faded
at the same time
        that other religious practices
                from pagan nations
were filtering into Israel.

During this time,
there was a woman by the name of Hannah,
who was found to be childless
after several years of marriage.

She and her husband were devout.
In this,
they were among the last of their kind.

Every year
they would go to worship the Lord
              in the tent where the Ark was kept,
but so bitter was Hannah's childlessness--
so reproachful to her
that she would weep
and refuse to eat.

After one such paroxysm of grief
              during a meal with her husband
she rose from the table
and presented herself before the Lord
              in the temple.
In her bitterness she wept
and poured out her prayer:

> *"O Lord of Hosts, if you will look on the misery of*
> *your handmaid, if you will remember me and do*
> *not forget your handmaid but give to your hand-*
> *maid a male child, I will give him to the Lord for*
> *as long as he lives."*   1 Samuel 1:11

As she continued to pray quietly before the Lord,
the priest Eli observed her.

He thought that she was drunk and said to her:

> *"How long will you make a drunken spectacle of*
> *yourself? Put away your wine."*
>   1 Samuel 1:14

But Hannah answered:

> *"No, my Lord, I am an unhappy woman. I have*
> *drunk neither wine nor strong drink.*

I have been pouring out my troubles before the Lord. Do not regard your handmaid as a worthless woman for I have been speaking out of my great anguish and my misery."

cf. 1 Samuel 1:15

Then Eli answered,

"Go in peace, and may the God of Israel grant you what you have asked of him."

1 Samuel 1:17

Hannah rose up,
changed by the encounter with the priest.

In spite of Eli's hasty judgment,
she accepted the dismissal of the priest
        as a word of affirmation from God,
and his blessing as a sign
        that God had heard the prayer
which poured out
from the deepest place within her.

She was emptied now of her grief.
All of its toxin,
all of its sorrow was given to God
        as a prayer,
        as a lamentation in faith,
and she believed that God had heard her.

How important it is to offer to God,
to pour out to him
that which is within.

When we live with thanksgiving,
                rather than with bitterness,
                rather than with self-absorption,
when we live with gratitude,
                rather than with fear and complaint,
when we live the Eucharistic life,
then we are able
to be filled with the blessings of God;
blessings that prior to that time
                we were closed to receive:
blessings of release;
blessings of mutuality;
blessings of future hopes fulfilled.

Hannah bore a son
                whose name was Samuel.
She had dedicated him to God from the womb,
and true to her words,
delivered him
                to the service of the temple
                        when he was merely a child,
scarcely old enough to walk.

He became the errand boy
of the priest who had given her the blessing.

Hannah made a return to the Lord
                of the life which had been given to her.
The boy grew up and became the prophet
who restored Israel to faith,
        anointed kings,
and called upon David
to rise up to the service of God
and restore the nation to his Covenant.

Every promise of the Covenant
flowed through Hannah's prayer,
and then through Hannah's son.

When Hannah brought Samuel to the temple
            and surrendered him,
she surrendered
            that which was most precious to her.
In so doing,
she thereby surrendered herself as well
to God's unfolding will.

When we give away the gift
            which is most precious to us,
we give ourselves away to God;
we invite his will to be done.

When Hannah left her son at the temple, she prayed:

> *"My heart exalts in the Lord,*
>   *my strength is exalted in my God.*
> *I have swallowed up my enemies;*
>   *I rejoice in my victory.*
> *There is no Holy One like the Lord,*
>   *there is no Rock like our God.*
>
> *The bows of the mighty are broken,*
>   *but the feeble gird on strength.*
> *The well-fed have hired themselves out*
>   *for bread,*
>   *while the hungry are fat with spoils.*
> *The barren wife bears seven sons,*
>   *while the mother of many languishes.*

The Lord puts to death and gives life.
he casts down to the nether world;
he raises up again.
The Lord makes poor and makes rich.
he humbles, he also exalts.
He raises up the poor from the dust.
1 Samuel 2:1-8

That was Hannah's song of praise
which followed upon her earlier prayer
in which she had surrendered the child she longed for
in tears--
her "fiat" in the temple.

Her prayer life can be divided neatly
between two moments:
"fiat" and "magnificat."

"Fiat" is the outpouring of the heart in trust.

"Magnificat" is the praising
and the thanking of God
because God himself
is cause enough for thanksgiving.

What did Hannah gain by the birth of her son?

She surrendered him to God
while he was still a child.

She was thanking God because of God,
she was recounting his deeds,
                his works,
                his power.
Her heart was filled with God
rather than with the problems of her own soul.

Hannah bears reference to the Eucharistic life,
                        to the life of thanksgiving.
Her magnificat was her prayer of gratitude,
the sign of a heart outpoured in reverence
                for the gift which God is,
for the gifts which he gave.

There is an interesting parallel
between Hannah's surrender
and that of Miriam,
the sister of Moses,
who lived several centuries earlier.

Because the Hebrews in Egypt were increasing
                in great numbers,
Pharaoh ordered
        that all male children born to them
be put to death.

In an attempt to preserve the life of her son,
the mother of Miriam,
Jochebed,
placed him in a basket,
                an "ark," so-called,
amid the reeds along the Nile.

Miriam stationed herself at a distance
to watch over the child,
to see what would become of him.

She kept vigil
following the ark,
silently, at the river's edge
        as she waited for Providence
to bring about what God intended,
even as one day
Israel would follow another ark
        for forty years
in the desert.

When Pharaoh's daughter came to the river
to bathe
and discovered the basket
        and the babe within it,
Miriam came forward
    and offered to find a woman
to nurse him for the princess.

She willingly surrendered her brother
        to Pharaoh's daughter
thereby allowing his life
to be miraculously preserved
because of her openness and acceptance
        of the will of God.

Like Hannah,
    who surrendered what was dear to her,
Miriam became the instrument
        through which God's power
shaped the destiny of his people.

Miriam disappeared from the scene at this point.

She appears several chapters later
                in the Book of Exodus
at the epic moment
                when Moses stretched out his staff
and parted the Red Sea.

She was now once again with Moses--
whose life was reborn
                when he was lifted up
                        from the waters of the Nile.
She was now at his side
while a whole nation was being born
        as they passed through the waters
of the Red Sea.

When the Hebrews arrived safely
                on the other side,
Moses and the Israelites
sang a song of thanksgiving
to the Lord.

Miriam took a tambourine in her hand
and,
leading all the women with tambourines,
danced along the seashore,
singing this refrain:

> "*Sing to the Lord, for he is gloriously
>   triumphant;
> horse and chariot he has cast into the sea.*"
>   Exodus 15:21

Miriam was twice on the edge of the abyss,
            twice on the edge of the waters of death.
In both cases
she was present
to celebrate the mystery of life:
first, as a "fiat,"
to provide a moment of grace
            whereby the daughter of Pharaoh
would save the life of the child Moses.

She was present next
as a "magnificat,"
        at the edge of the Red Sea
with a tambourine in her hand
        celebrating,
        leaping,
        dancing for joy,
because God had delivered
not only one child
            from death in a river
but a whole nation
            from slavery
as they passed through the Red Sea.

Another Old Testament woman
            of great faith
was a widow by the name of Judith.

Judith lived many centuries after Hannah
            in one of the villages
on the outskirts of Jerusalem.

She had great zeal,
and dedication to God in the temple,
that is,
for the Ark of the Covenant
over which dwelt the presence of God
in the temple.

When her husband died,
she was left with the charge of his estate,
and according to the Book of Judith,
she was a woman of sterling qualities.

Judith remained a widow at home
where she set up a tent for herself
                on the roof of her house.
She lived in the tent just as her ancestors did
who,
like Abraham and Sarah,
were shepherds and nomads--
a life of great purity,
        great zeal,
great trust in God.

She lived a life
which resembled the journey of Israel
        when they left Egypt
and traveled for forty years
in the desert.

She put sackcloth around her waist,
and dressed in the clothing of a widow.

She fasted all the days of her widowhood
except the day before the Sabbath
                    and the Sabbath itself
on the day of the new moon
and the festival days
of the House of Israel.

Only when the community rejoiced
did she rejoice
because she had in her heart
          the welfare of her people,
rather than her own career
and her own well-being.

Her life coincided with that of the community,
just as her body lived in a tent
and coincided with the foundation
          of its national origin,
as a people on the move.

She lived for them,
          with them,
and in prayer on their behalf.

She was a contemplative
who carried in her heart
the burden of the community.

Judith was beautiful in appearance,
          lovely to behold.
No one spoke ill of her
for she feared God with great devotion.

It was during the lifetime of Judith
      that the city of Jerusalem was attacked.
It was besieged by the enemy
and was about to fall.

Judith heard
      that the elders of the city
were ready to surrender,
and she may well have thought to herself:

> "This must not be.
> We must not surrender Zion
> because it contains the temple of the Lord
> and within the temple
> is the Ark of God's Covenant--
> God's very presence.
> It must never be that we surrender it
> for our own benefit."

Judith sent her maid to the elders
      to ask them to visit her.
When they came,
she said to them:

> *"Therefore, my brothers, let us set an example*
> *for our kinsmen. Their lives depend upon us and*
> *the defense of the sanctuary; the temple and the*
> *altar rest upon us."*   Judith 8:24

She continued:

> *"In spite of everything, let us give thanks to the*
> *Lord our God who is putting us to the test as he*
> *did our ancestors."*   cf. Judith 8:25

Judith knew something of her ancestors;
she lived their lives
in the tent on the roof of her house.

She continued:

> *"Remember how he dealt with Abraham and how*
> *he tested Isaac; he has not tried us with fire as he*
> *did them to search their hearts, nor has he taken*
> *vengeance on us, but the Lord chastises those who*
> *are close to him in order to admonish them. . . .*
> *Let me pass through the gate with my maid tonight,*
> *and within the days you have specified, the Lord*
> *will rescue Israel by my hand."*
>
> cf. Judith 8:26-27,33

The leader of the elders
gave her leave to go
with these words:

> *"Go in peace, and may the Lord God go before*
> *you to take vengeance upon our enemies!"*
>
> Judith 8:35

After praying at length
        to the Lord God
while incense was being offered in the temple
                        that evening,
Judith went down into her house.

She dressed in her festive attire,
        anointed herself with rich ointment,
and put on her jewelry
to captivate the eyes
of all who would see her.

Then she and her maid
passed through the gate of the city
and walked across the valley
            into the camp of the enemy.

She was escorted by the guards
            to the tent of Holofernes
who was immediately enthralled
by her beauty.

Judith stayed in the camp three days.

In the night watch before each dawn
she went outside the camp with her maid
to pray to the Lord to direct her way,
then returned to her tent.

Then, on the fourth day,
Holofernes invited her to come to his tent
for a great banquet.

In the course of the feasting,
the general drank a great quantity of wine--
more than he had ever drunk
            on a single day in his life.

When it grew late,
everyone withdrew from the tent
as they were all tired
            from the prolonged festivities
of the banquet.

141

When all the guests had departed
Judith was left alone with Holofernes
who lay prostrate on his bed
sodden with wine.

After praying to the Lord for strength,
Judith beheaded him with his own sword.

She gave his head to her maid
who put it in her pouch.

They then walked quietly out of the camp
as if going to their place of prayer.

When reaching the city of Zion
Judith shouted to the guards
to open the gate.

She then showed the head of Holofernes
          to the people and the elders
who had gathered there
when they heard her voice.

> The high priest Joakim and the elders who lived in
> Jerusalem came to witness the good things that the
> Lord had done for Israel, and to see Judith and to
> wish her well. When they met her, they blessed her
> with one accord and said to her:
>
> > "You are the glory of Jerusalem,
> >   the surpassing joy of Israel,
> >   you are the splendid boast of our people.
> > What you have done with your own hands
> >   you have done good to Israel.

God is pleased with what you have
    wrought.
May you be blessed by the Lord Almighty
    forever and ever!"

And all the people shouted, "Amen."
                             cf. Judith 15:8-10

She took branches in her hands and distributed them to the women around her. They crowned themselves with olive wreaths and she went before all the people leading all the women in a dance, while all the men of Israel followed in their armor, wearing garlands and singing hymns.
                             cf. Judith 15:12-13

Just like Miriam of old
who led the women folk in a dance
on the Red Sea shore,
Judith led all Israel in a song of thanksgiving
with these words:

    "Strike up the instruments,
        a song to my God with timbrels
        chant to the Lord with cymbals;
    Sing to him a new song,
        exult and acclaim his name.

    For the Lord is God; he crushes
        warfare.
    and sets his encampment among
        his people;
    he snatched me from the hands
        of my persecutors.

    The Lord Almighty thwarted them,
        by a woman's hand he confounded
        them.

"Not by youths was their mighty one
struck down
nor did titans bring him low,
nor huge giants attack him;
But Judith, by the beauty of her
countenance disabled him.
She took off her widow's garb to
raise the afflicted in Israel.
She anointed her face with fragrant oil,
with a tiara she fastened her
tresses."
She put on a linen robe to beguile him.
Her sandals caught his eyes,
and her beauty captivated his mind.
The sword cut through his neck."

Judith 16: 1-2,5-9

A very strong and amazing hymn
about this prayerful widow
of great beauty and heroism.

The song continued:

"A new hymn I will sing to my God.
O Lord, great are you and glorious,
wonderful in power and
unsurpassable.
Let your every creature serve you;
for you spoke, and they were made.
You sent forth your spirit, and they
were created;
no one can resist your word.
The mountains to their bases, and the
seas are shaken;
the rocks, like wax, melt before
your glance."

Judith 16:13-15

It's a long hymn,
this magnificat,
this song of thanksgiving.

But there was also in Judith a fiat.

In her widowhood
she was not filled with bitterness
                    and lamentation,
denouncing the Providence of God.

In her widowhood
she was not filled with self-pity,
but she pitched a tent on the roof of her house
so that she might live in God's presence.

She was filled with devotion
and she persuaded the elders of her race
to faith.

She lived her fiat;
she poured herself out in prayer.

She was a woman of surrender,
and then, alternatively,
she was a woman of Eucharistic prayer,
                    and thanksgiving.

She tells us,
     "In all things, let us give thanks to God,"
even as she learned to give thanks
alone in the tent,
on the roof her house.

These are the two great themes
of the spiritual life:
"fiat" and "magnificat."

Both of them are brought together
in the Eucharistic life of Christ Jesus
who,
on the night before he died,
offered his magnificat to God
            in Eucharistic thanksgiving
at the Passover meal.

Later,
in the garden
that same evening,
he also offered up his body
in obedience and surrender
to the will of his Father
and in submission to the needs,
                        the weakness,
                        the sorrow
and the sin of our race.

"This is my body,"
  he said,
          then,
"Not my will, but yours be done."

In one Eucharistic night
there rose up from the lips of our Savior
a "fiat" and a "magnificat"--
the two great themes of prayer.

146

Whether we pray our devotions
        in that mind
        and in that mentality,
or we pray centering prayer,
or spontaneous prayer,
or charismatic prayer,
whatever the manner of our praying,
we are only praying
if we are suspended between these two themes:
        "surrender and thanksgiving,"
        "fiat and magnificat."

Eucharistic prayer is the prayer
        that Jesus offered
day and night
at the Father's side.

And into that prayer
he gathers his Church
        around the altar
        and in the tent
of our own personal prayer.

VII

Gifts in Due Season

*O*nce more will I set forth my theme
        to shine like the moon in its
                fullness!
Listen, my faithful children: open up
        your petals,
        like roses planted near running
                waters;
Send up the sweet fragrance of incense,
        break forth in blossoms like the lily
Send up the sweet odor of your hymn
        of praise;
        bless the Lord for all he has done!
Proclaim the greatness of his name,
        loudly sing his praises,
With music on the harp and all
        stringed instruments;
        sing out with joy as you proclaim:
The works of God are all of them good;
        in its own time every need is
                supplied.

                        Sirach 39:12-16

The ancient sage
uses an illustration from nature
to express his desire
        to witness to the truth of God's goodness.
He wishes to be like the moon
which finally shows forth
its full light.

Then he asks us to be like the roses
which open up their petals
        to the sun
or to the moonlight of his testimony.

He wants the listeners
to accept
        the generous gift of his words
and to be drawn into friendship
with God.

He asks us to be like the lily
with its sweet fragrance
wafting up to heaven.

The author of Sirach
uses these illustrations from nature
to elicit a response;
to say to the children of Israel
and to say to us:

        "Lilies and roses and moons
         know how to give evidence
         that they are God's,
         that they belong to him.

        "Give evidence also,
         like lilies and roses and moons;
         obey and respond to God's word.

        "Do so yourself,
         freely;
         do so yourself,
         willingly.

        "God invites you.
         Proclaim his greatness."

Sirach tells us
that all of the works of God are good.

One of the reasons
that we should be praising and thanking God,
says the ancient sage,
is because
he provides for our needs in time,
in due season.

In the proper moment
he supplies what is necessary for us.

One of the reasons we forget
to give God thanks,
or we neglect to,
is because we are distracted by the idea
        that we are missing something
        that we need here and now.
In the lack of what we want,
we become so absorbed and preoccupied
that we forget to be grateful to God
for what we have.

So the sage is at pains to persuade us
that no matter what we think we lack,
        no matter what we feel we miss
we have sufficient gifts from God
in this time and in this season
        right now
to offer up
the fragrance of our praise
the music of our gratitude,
the brilliance of our witness,
the light of our charity.

We have what is necessary
to give to God
 a generous display of thanksgiving,
   an honest display of gratitude
for his gifts.

We ought not to play an unworthy game
with God--
that if he gives us what we require
in addition to everything else
                    that he has given,
if he gives what we require
        here and now,
then we will give him something in return
        here and now.

God has given us everything we need
and continues to generously supply us
                in due season.

Our response ought to be uncalculated
and boundless.

Our gratitude should be sincere
and without reservation.

Such are the kind of responses
we gave to the grace of God
if we accepted the gift of marriage.

At the altar,
before our families and before God
      all the angels and saints
      and the witness of the Church,
we said things like:
          "In sickness and health,
          in good times and bad,
          for richer and poorer,
          till death do us part."

We said extraordinary things,
         heroic things,
         dramatic things.
We had been living absolutely bland,
                  pedestrian,
                  blasé lives.
But when we walked down the aisle
         of that church
the foundations of the world were shaking.

We declared things
      which were altogether immoderate.

We made an offering.

Or if we made a Religious Profession
      of Evangelical Poverty, Chastity and Obedience,
we accepted the grace
to live in community life
to live without the security
         of personal possessions
without the consolation of spouse
without the affirmation of children.

If we professed those vows
the pillars of the Church were shaking,
half in fear and half in joy,
      that anybody
should ever make such a promise.

The most important promises of all
were made when we were baptized.

"Do you reject Satan?"

Imagine this!

Mere flesh that we are,
fighting combat against Satan
and saying once and for all,

"Yes! I do reject him!"

"And all his pomps?
 And all his empty promises?"

"Yes!" we said,
      or our sponsors said for us.
"Yes! We reject them."

And then,
"Do you believe in God, the Father Almighty
and Christ Jesus his only Son?
Do you believe in a love so great
that it conquers death and raises you up
to the face of God?"

"Yes," we said, "we believe."

"Do you believe in a Church,
in a communion of such grace and love,
that no matter what you see to the contrary,
    no matter how disillusioned you get with it,
    no matter how it burns you,
do you still believe?"

 "Yes," we said.

All the powers of hell were afraid
        when we were baptized
and "yes" was said,
    "fiat" was said
for us.

So we shone for a moment like a moon
                    in its brilliance
and we sent up our fragrance to heaven
        like a lily
and we opened up the petals of our heart
        like a rose.

Sweet incense filled the earth
every time we said "fiat,"
every time we accepted the drama
        of our lives.

This was our "magnificat."

Our lives are not boring,
                        tedious affairs.
They are dramas,
            poetic sagas,
            overwhelming mysteries.

They are worthy of novels
                    and epics
                    and movies,
or sometimes, just soap operas.

And oftentimes
we may have even heard ourselves say
that were we to have written it down in a book
nobody would have believed it.

That is to say,
that our lives are even greater
                than the literature of great lives,
greater--not necessarily better
                            or more virtuous
but weighty,
        substantial,
        serious.

What does God ask from us
when he asks for our love?

He asks for something
    which is weighty,
                substantial,
            and serious.

We might understand why God says
that he is a "jealous" God and "angry"
if we have *substantial* anxiety
        and *substantial* worry
        and *substantial* grief
        and *serious* concerns
about so many other things.

But, then, when it comes to our Faith
we have something like a casual regard
            for God,
an occasional regard for his love
an incidental,
    half-hearted practice
of our religion.

Well, then, God is a jealous God.

We have such constant aggravation,
                    and irritation
                    and anguish
                        about our children.
We have such constant concern and interest
in our financial reports.

Well, then, he's jealous.

How come they get so much attention
when he gets so little?

He doesn't want to be our hobby.
He doesn't want to be our avocation.

Very serious promises were made.

He wrote them down.

They're in a book.

Somebody said "Yes!"
Somebody said "Fiat!"

So he keeps looking to see
when we are going to open up
          the petals of our hearts
to his grace.

When are we going to send up the fragrance
          of the lily of our soul?

When are we going to shine forth like the moon
          in its brilliance?

He keeps waiting.

If these unintelligent elements of nature
know what to do on their own,
then why don't we--
who have been given all of nature
                    and all of grace--
why don't we do better
than they?

God has given us in our seasons
all that is necessary
for our lives.

That means,
of course,
that he doesn't give us everything
all at once.

Seasons require
that there is a dispersion of gifts
        each in its own special time,
one after the other.

We wait
as we follow a course,
            a process
and the gifts continue to flow.

Many of you remember the time
                when there was a seasonal diet.

When I was a child
        I could almost guess
what week of the summer it was
based upon the kind of strawberries
        or the kind of peach
which was then available
in the grocery store.

I could guess more or less
what time of the summer it was
by the kind and the quality of the tomato
that came in from the garden.

I no longer can make those distinctions
because we can get strawberries from Chile
                    and kiwi from Australia
in January.

We can have all kinds of fruits and vegetables
from every season under the sun
at any time of the year.

We have succeeded in spoiling ourselves very well.

God still has seasonal fruits for us.
There are gifts we cannot have today
that he reserves for tomorrow.

But we want everything all at once;
it is the spoiled child in us.

We can tell when children are spoiled
because they kick and scream
and flail their arms.

We are just like them
        more often than not,
except that we have learned
not to kick and scream
so obviously.

We whine instead.

We complain,
or we subtract from our prayer
the investment of our heart.

We subtract from God
the gift of our gratitude and thanksgiving.
But God sees the kicking,
                    screaming child within us.

Other people may think
that we are quite sincere and mature.

We can carry on a fine pretense
before our spouse,
          our children
        and our friends.

But God knows
          that many times
we have scarcely grown
from the spoiled child we once were.

He gives to each of us his fruits in due season.

Life, then,
is a continual discovery
          of the fruit that God gives us
each day,
and a continual surrender
of last season's gifts.

Life is a constant openness
          to the blessings
          that God wishes to give
and a constant letting go
of the gifts we had formerly enjoyed.

Aging is such a process
        of being open to new gifts
and letting go of old ones.

The author of the Book of Sirach
has chosen Nature
                as a theme for faith
quite wisely,
for Nature provides a constant rotation
of the seasons.

Little seasons and great seasons.
Long seasons and short seasons.

The night and the day--
the two seasons that are repeated so often
        that we have become regularized
by them.

We are rather closely conjoined
to these seasons of dark and light,
so much so
that many people actually enjoy the summer
                        with a good mood
and suffer the winter with a bad one.

Many of us are seasonally affected
more than we know.

164

It is a good thing for us
in October and November
            while the sun still shines
to walk in it for a moment or two
every day.

We need to enjoy this blessing of God
            before the winter arrives
and the shadows lengthen
and we have no opportunity in the cold
to enjoy the natural light
of the sun.

Then the mood will darken
and the temper flare;
then we'll want more and more sleep
as depression sets in.

Day and night are seasons built into our lives.

The moon and its quarters
are also seasonal,
monthly.

As an anthropologist,
I have two figurines
at Saint Vincent College
that I use as examples in my classes.

They are among the oldest statues
that human beings have ever made.

165

They are both female figurines
just a few inches tall
and both of them are extraordinarily proportioned
what we would consider oversexed:
      large,
      corpulent,
      abundant,
almost grotesque.

Anthropologists believe
that they were in some sense
      fertility figurines;
that men and women who wanted more children
would employ them in their rituals,
in their prayers and in their sacrifices.

Or, if they wanted more offspring
      in the herds that they were following,
they might implore these figurines
that there should be more abundant life.

Not so long ago
it was noticed
that there were notches
carved at various places on the figurines,
in a series of scratches.

No one paid much attention to them
for a long time.

They had just imagined
      that over the years
there was some deterioration,
some marring of the art,
some vandalism.

But when they counted the notches,
          in almost every case
they discovered
that the notches were numbered
in sets of twenty-eight.

Ah!
Twenty-eight!
A month.
A lunar month.

The seasons of the moon
and the season of fertility.

Twenty, thirty thousand years ago
human beings noticed
that there was a remarkable correspondence
          between heaven and earth.
The cycle of the moon and its phases
matched exactly the cycle of fertility!

No wonder, then,
that on the image of a fertility goddess
notches were carved
which number the phases of the moon.

Heaven and earth in a seasonal alliance.

One of the great themes of religion
is that we should have on earth
a correspondence to the order
and the mystery of heaven.

"Thy will be done on earth as it is in heaven."

Our life on earth
should follow the pattern
and obey the will
of the sovereignty of God in heaven.

Human beings on earth
should say "yes"
        like the moon says "yes"
and the stars following their courses
say "yes."

We in our marriages and in our families
                        and our relationships
should say "yes,"
        just as the bodies of heaven
obediently follow the design of their Maker.

There are other seasonal patterns:
the four seasons of the year
        that we enjoy
in this temperate climate.

Or the seasons of life itself:
        birth,
        maturation,
        decline
and death.

There are so many kinds of seasons
that go around and around.

There are so many kinds of seasons
which make of the circle of life
            an endless loop
of time.

Almost all the religions of the world
have been entranced
        by the idea of seasons.
Almost all of them have been seduced
by meditation on this subject.

It's overwhelming and mysterious
            that we,
            like nature,
are gathered up in a symphony
which rises and falls in a regular pattern.

It's awesome and haunting
and it shows the mark of the Creator.

Christianity,
like all the religions of the world
sees this correspondence
        of heaven and earth.
Christians,
likewise,
        have this intuition.
But our intuition
goes deeper into the matter
and understands more of the substance
                    of the mystery
than do any of the others.

169

Our insight travels further
into the bond of heaven and earth.

For we believe
that it is not just a rotation of the seasons
                    that we perceive,
not just a routine that is followed.

But, rather
we see in the cycles
            of day and night
                sun and moon;
we see in the seasons
            of spring and summer,
                autumn and winter,
  the cycle of life and death--
we see in all of these changes
the mystery of self-emptying love
and sacrifice.

These cycles are not just a natural process,
                    not just a blind mechanism;
they are an evidence
of something in the heart of God
that is filled with love
and willing to outpour itself.

All of the elements of nature
show a willingness to pour themselves out
                    to give themselves up
                    and to let themselves go
so that new life can emerge.

170

The old moon dies
        so that the new moon
can come into being.

The clouds above us
must yield their moisture
or there will be no rain for life below.

The earth beneath our feet
must yield its nutrients
or there will be no plants.

The leaves in the green of summer
yield to a glorious dying
        in the beauty of autumn.
The fall yields its glory
        to the purity of winter.
Winter yields its purity
        to the promise of life in spring
and this promise gives way
        to fulfillment
in the fruit of summer.

Each season dies,
        lets go,
and pours itself out
so that another season
can come to be.

A youth will never mature
        unless he gives himself away
in a loving relationship.

But a loving relationship
      will never mature into a saving bond
unless it opens itself up to parenting.

Parents will never be good parents
      unless they learn to let go
little by little
of the children they cling to.

All these things must give themselves up
as the day yields to night
      and gives us sleep.
All good things allow themselves
      in their goodness
to die.

What did Jesus say?

    *"Unless the seed falls to the ground and dies, it
    remains just a single grain, but if it dies, if it
    disintegrates, it yields abundant fruit, a harvest."*
                         cf. John 12:24

When Christianity
looks at the seasons of the year
it is an act of generosity
      that it sees
and not just the rhythm of change.

It is an act of sacrifice and self-emptying
      that it sees
and not just a rotation
      from one thing to another.

Above all,
we see in God,
          in the mystery of the Trinity,
the origin and cause
of all the seasons of the year.

All the phases of the sun
                and the moon and stars,
all the cycles of life and death
are mirrored in the perfect drama
of the Father
who empties himself out,
          lets himself go,
and surrenders himself over to the Son.

The Son receives
all that the Father has to give
and responds to him
          with an equal gift of self
as he pours himself back
into the heart of his Father.

We see in Christ Jesus the analog
of the mystery of life and death,
          of letting go,
of surrendering and being born anew.

Through his self-emptying love,
Christ surrenders to the season of dying
          that there might be for us
a season of life.

From his side flows blood and water,
the fountain of the sacramental life
               of his Church.

Christ Jesus
has gathered us into the same process--
not just a mechanism,
               but in a dynamism of love
not just a rotation,
but in the mystery of faith and trust in God.

In the Near East
in the region of Palestine
there are two seas,
two large inland bodies of water.

They are more or less of the same size;
they both have more or less the same climate
and they both are fed
by the River Jordan.

So in every respect it would seem
that they would be
about the same kind of sea.

But the one sea,
the Sea of Galilee
is filled with life,
life in abundance,
with fish that have served every generation
for many thousands of years.

It is a sea in which people recreate with joy
and around which people live for refreshment
and sustenance.

But the other sea, the Dead Sea,
is so saline,
so mineralized
        that nothing lives in its waters.
It is the lowest place on earth.

The reason that this sea is dead
                while the other is alive
is that the Sea of Galilee
receives water from one direction
and pours it out in a river
        in the other.

It receives and it gives.

The Dead Sea,
by contrast,
so low does it lie
that it can only receive the water
        of the Jordan River;
nothing flows out from it.

The water that flows in
must seep slowly into the abyss below
or evaporate from its surface.

It yields nothing to anyone.

175

And so the Sea of Galilee and the Dead sea
provide a good illustration
                    of what course
our lives may follow.

God is giving us gifts in their course
          but if we are dying inwardly
              if we are yielding no fruit for anyone
              if we have no life in us,
it might well be
because we are pouring nothing out
          we are offering nothing up
letting nothing go.

We have kept every gift for ourselves.

If we are anxious
          overwrought,
     and self-absorbed,
then we are like the Dead Sea.

But if we are gracious,
          and trusting
          and generous
and we let flow out from us
all the gifts that flow in
          without measure
          without reservation,
then we will be live-filled
and life-giving.

176

So when we survey all the wonders of creation,
when we walk through the autumn foliage
     and look at death glorious,
                 afire,
let us listen to what the ancient sage
     has invited us to hear.
Let us accept an obedience
     for ourselves
which corresponds to his testimony.

The works of God are all of them good
     every need when it comes he fills.
No cause then to say: "This is not as
     good as that";
     for each shows its worth at the
     proper time.
So now with full joy of heart proclaim
     and bless the name of the Holy One.
                     Sirach 39:33-35

VIII

Gifts of Bread and Wine

Genesis describes at some length
          the mentality,
          the attitude of thanksgiving
                    in the life of Abraham,
about how
when he was returning in triumph
          after liberating his nephew
          from the kings
                    who had taken him hostage,
his first and his greatest act
was to offer up gratitude to God,
     to acknowledge the help of God
publicly.

He did this
          through the services of a priest,
an obscure and mysterious personage
                    called Melchizedek
who suddenly appeared on the scene
at that moment.

It was an extraordinary engagement,
because hitherto
Abraham had been able to offer up his own
thanksgiving to God
          with Sarah
without the services of a priest.

Abraham traveled with Sarah
all across the length
          and breadth of Israel.

They worshipped
    on mountain heights,
       under trees that were signs of the Covenant,
             like the terebinth of Mamre,
     by wells of water
             like the seven springs at Beersheba--
places
where God's Covenant was made visible
        through the waters of a fountain
or the shade of a tree.

They were able to offer up their thanksgiving
 on altars they had constructed themselves,
with fires they had lit themselves,
      with animal offerings and sacrifices
they had prepared themselves.

But at this moment
Abraham seemed to require the services
     of someone else
        to offer up a sacrifice.
He did not rely upon his own royal priesthood.

He called upon the sacerdotal office
     of this mysterious figure Melchizedek,
because apparently
there is that reality
    that even Abraham acknowledged:
    that finally and ultimately,
we are not able of ourselves
        to fully offer
what we wish to give to God.

It was the Psalmist
who raised the rhetorical question
which must have been at the heart
            of Abraham's engagement
with Melchizedek:

> *How can I make a return to the Lord*
> *   for all the good he had done for me?*
> *The cup of salvation I will take up,*
> *   and I will call on the name of the Lord.*
>   Psalm 116:12-13

The Psalmist inquired
as to what manner
he could make the gift of himself to God
                        in thanksgiving,
and he was frustrated
            by the limitations of his capacity
to offer that gift.

Much of the time
we are frustrated
            by our inability
to make offerings
which match our intentions.

There are people we would like to persuade
                        of how lovable they are;
there are people
            to whom we would like to declare our love
                        and have them believe it,
but we have not been able
to find the words which declare it,
or the gesture which makes it obvious.

We continually struggle to keep finding,
                    to keep expressing
the means by which we can make it clear
and certain
          how we stand in relationship to them.

There is a tremendous frustration in being human
                              in this regard.

We are too much locked up
                    within ourselves,
too much trapped.

Our ideas,
our intentions,
our desires are not plainly visible,
so we must find the art--
really it is an art--
          of making what is interior
                              exterior;
          of making the interior gift
                    an external offering;
                    the interior generosity
an external oblation.

Even Abraham sought help in this regard;
he sought a priest
                    to make known his gratitude to God.

We should pay attention
          to the humility of Abraham
who exercised his full faculties,
yet acknowledged his limits.

He sought the art of another's mission,
          the art of another's ministry
to complete his worship
and to fulfill his thanksgiving.

We should pay attention to Abraham
because we live in a society
               in which there is a strong tendency
to try to become self-sufficient
               in every respect,
not to require others
     to round ourselves out.

We want every gift to be our gift--
               ours alone
and personally.

When women tell me
that being a priest is the fullness
          of being a Catholic
and therefore it should not be reserved to men,
I can only answer that statement
               by the very same logic:
that every child who is baptized
should then also be ordained
so that no one is deprived
          of the fullness
of being a Catholic.

But I do not think
          that everyone should be ordained
at Baptism.

I do think that we as baptized persons
should acknowledge our limits,
        acknowledge even with a certain relief
that we do not have everything,
nor can we offer up everything to God
                by ourselves
alone.

We need Christ Jesus
to make the offering of ourselves
                to the Father.
We are not an acceptable offering
                without him.
We have not the power to give ourselves to God
apart from him.

There is in the Church
various aspects of his mission
                and his charisms,
various aspects of his person
reflected in the varied prisms
        of individual lives
and souls.

Some reflect the chastity of Christ
                by their Religious vows.
Some reflect the poverty of Christ
                by their care for the homeless.
Some reflect the obedience of Christ
                by their fidelity to the will of God.
Some reflect the voice of Christ
                by their prophetic call.

Some are priests
    and reflect his ministry as High Priest,
                on the Cross,
and at the Eucharistic table.

To each is given various gifts
          and tasks
          and purposes
so as to make up the fullness of Christ.

To paraphrase the words of St. Paul:
    "No one is given every gift, so that we will rely
    upon each other, and that by enjoying the witness,
    the charism of one another, the whole Church is
    knit together as so many members of the one
    Body."   cf. 1 Corinthians

We are knit together in praise,
            and thanksgiving
that such a Body we may belong to
and in that Body
we may be offered up to God.

Echoing the words of Adam,
Christ Jesus can say of his Body, the Church:
    "This one, at last, is flesh of my flesh and bone
       of my bones."

He says this of us
and we can be grateful
            that we are received;
            that we are the object of divine delight;
            that we are accepted and embraced
                              by the Risen Savior.
We are members of the Body he has called his Bride
and named as his own.

We need his service,
            his priesthood,
and the art of his self-offering
to make the halting,
            fearful
            and anxious desires
                        of our inmost being
pure desires of self-surrender to God.

To that end,
we are required to align ourselves
            with the offering of Christ
in his Paschal Mysteries.

This is what Abraham began to intuit
                  when he returned from his victory.

Abraham was met by Melchizedek--
            this obscure priest of the Most High God,
            this king of Salem--
as he was returning
from defeating the kings of the north.

And to him
Abraham apportioned one-tenth
of everything he had gained
as his offering of thanksgiving.

By giving up one-tenth of all the spoils,
Abraham was saying:

"These are not mine first.
These are not mine most.
I received them from God.
They came from God.
It was God who won the victory.
It was God who gave me the gifts.
They are his.
To acknowledge where they have come from,
I hereby offer to God
one-tenth of the booty
as a gesture,
as a sign of recognition and gratitude."

But Melchizedek also gave something to Abraham.

There was a gift exchange.
There was a mutual engagement.
There was reciprocity.

Melchizedek gave Abraham bread and wine:
a thanksgiving offering.
Abraham ate and drank with Melchizedek
the gifts
which God gave him in return.

189

Why bread and wine?
What do bread and wine symbolize?

Long before the Last Supper,
universally,
bread and wine had a clear significance
to peoples everywhere.

The bread is brown,
but under the surface it is white.

Baked in the oven,
it is brown on the outside,
but that part on the inside
            which is not near the flame
is of a lighter color and texture.

It is just like human flesh.

Certainly in ancient times
the skin of a man,
            baked by the sun,
was brown on the surface,
but lighter underneath--
paler, even white.

In every society
the folklore,
the fables,
the myth of human creation
are all the same.

190

In the beginning,
as the stories go,
human beings were baked in an oven
and the gods opened the door of the oven
                        from time to time
and we can guess
which races were taken out first,
                                next
                    and last.

Peoples everywhere told these stories
                        about bread
because to them,
bread was like flesh.

Peoples everywhere told the same stories
                            about wine.
It is so dark,
    so rich
    and red,
that peoples everywhere saw
            in the crimson red of the wine
the very image of blood.

During our Civil War,
a song was sung
            about the trampling out the vintage
where the grapes of wrath were stored.

The poet was speaking of the blood of a nation
            which was being poured out
                    in battle after battle:
the grapes of wrath.

What was Melchizedek giving back to Abraham
         in return for the bounty that he offered?

By sharing bread and wine with him,
he was saying to Abraham:

    "God gave you more than your nephew Lot.
    God gave you more than the booty and the spoils,
    more than the fame and the reputation
    that you have gained,
    the notoriety and the stature
    of your success.
    God gave you your flesh and blood today.
    He preserved your life throughout the battle;
    he restored to you
    your own heart and soul,
    your body and your blood."

Abraham was enriched by the meditation.

God gave back his life
for risking his own life
for his nephew.

The Book of Numbers describes almost every kind
               of thanksgiving offering
which was ever given to God in Israel--
the kind of offerings
which were sacrificed on the altars of the temple
             and in the tent
in which the children of Israel worshipped God
for forty years.

The Lord instructed Moses to tell the Israelites:

> *"When you have entered the land that I will give you for your homesteads, if you make to the Lord a sweet-smelling oblation from the herd or from the flock, in holocaust, in fulfillment of a vow, or as a freewill offering, or for one of your festivals, whoever does so shall also present to the Lord a cereal offering consisting of one tenth of an ephah of fine flour mixed with a fourth of a hin of oil, as well as a libation of a fourth of a hin of wine, with each lamb sacrificed in holocaust or otherwise."*
>
> Numbers 15:2-5

There was an admixture of wheat and wine
       in every offering of the flesh and blood
              of every lamb,
              of every ram,
              of every ox.
Every animal, great or small
was offered to God with wheat and wine,
and so we remember the gift exchange
       of Abraham and Mclchizedek.

The intention of this ritual
was to remind the children of Israel
that ultimately
their thanksgiving was for life itself,
           for flesh and blood.

It was for thanksgiving for their mother's fidelity
           to the mystery of the life within her,
and thanksgiving for their father's fidelity
           which helped sustain that life
after it was born.

Fidelity to life,
            thanksgiving for flesh and blood.
This is what is symbolized
                    by bread and wine.
So we can more easily understand the transition
that our Savior made in the Passover meal
                    when bread and wine
became the central symbol of sacrifice.

No longer the lamb or the ram,
            the sheep or the goat,
            the ox or the bull,
but now bread and wine--
the image of flesh and blood--
are offered as the primary sign of a Covenant,
a Covenant sealed
            in the flesh and blood of Christ
under the image of bread and wine.

Like Abraham,
we likewise approach the Lord,
wondering how to make our offering
of thanksgiving.

What can we do?
How can we make a return to the Lord
for all that God has given to us--
especially for life itself?

What a poor gift we have to offer back!

God has given us our life.
What have we done with it?
How have we marred it?

How can we go into his presence
and offer what he gave us
                    pure and holy,
now smirched and disfigured so frequently
by our sin
and selfishness?

It is like the child
offering dandelions to his mother,
or as I did once,
            much worse,
offered goldenrods to my mother
who has many allergies.

And she received them,
                    I thought,
crying for joy,
and put them in a vase above the sink
for as long as I stayed in the kitchen
                    beaming over my little coup
by which I had bested my brother's dandelions
by my gift of goldenrods.

The gifts we have offered to God,
have, in fact,
            caused him many tears
and have wounded him deeply.

Yet he is able to receive our gifts
        in union with the body and blood of our Brother,
his beloved Son.

We give him what little good we have--
        that which is already his.
We give him back
        that which we have borrowed
           and have carelessly broken.
Yet he receives it
and gives us his Son,
        risen and living
        and life-giving to us
under the signs of bread and wine.

What a marvelous exchange!

The wonder and the joy
of participating in such a gift exchange as this
should be our primary source of love
           in this earthly life
and our primary source of hope
for the life to come.

Even before the time of Christ,
our ancestors in Israel
tried to offer up to God
some kind of gesture
        which would make vivid to them
their complete and utter reliance
upon the generosity of God.

They wanted to offer themselves--
their own flesh and blood,
but unable to do this
                without being destroyed by that very act,
they offered, instead, their animals,
                        great and small.

By destroying them
            and offering them as burnt holocausts,
they would say to God:

        "You are more important than our greatest wealth,
        our flocks and our herds.
        You are, in fact,
        the source of our very lives,
        our bodies and our blood."

The animals stood at the intersection
                        of their economy
                        and their biology.
They stood at the intersection
            of all that was God's best
and greatest gifts.

So they offered them
  as a sign of their own bodies
and a sign of their own economies.

For a thousand years,
the children of Israel offered up such sacrifices,
and they began to realize
            that the bodies of these animals
could be symbolized
        by bread and wine.

They began to mix in the blood
           the outpoured wine
and in with the flesh,
the wheat.

Christ continued this sacramental continuum
and made of his own body
           the intersection
                      of all of God's gifts
and made of his blood
           the intersection
of God's outpouring heart.

It is in the body and the blood of Christ
whereby all of the finest gifts of creation
                      and of human life,
           all of the finest gifts of God's generosity
meet
so that we can give
and God can give.

This gift exchange occurs in the Eucharist.

The bread and the wine are offered by the assembly
                      at the Offertory
as we place ourselves upon the altar
           in the bread and the wine
offered by the priest.

We offer the bread and the wine
like a tithe
        in thanksgiving
for all that God has done for us.

We offer the bread and the wine
in acknowledgment
            that even our bodies are from him.

We offer the bread and wine
for ourselves and for all the world--
                all the lives,
                    little and large,
                    great and small,
born and unborn.

And God accepts the offering,
really so poor,
        so humble
                    like a dandelion,
but he accepts it;
    he accepts it like a loving parent
who treasures a gift from a tiny child.

Indeed,
the good of it
                whatever there is
and the good will to give it
are already
his prior gifts to us.

But then in a moment,
he bestows upon us the unimaginable gift
in return:
the body and the blood of his own Son!

This is the gift
which matches all the desires of our heart:
to live in reciprocity
with God.

It releases from the deepest part of our soul
the wellspring of gratitude
and thanksgiving.

It releases from the depths of our being
all that we desire
to give to God.

ABOUT THE AUTHORS

Father Mark Gruber is a Benedictine monk of Saint Vincent Archabbey in Latrobe, Pennsylvania, who currently teaches classes in anthropology at Saint Vincent College. He received a B.A. in Philosophy and an M.Div. from Saint Vincent College and Seminary, as well as a Ph.D. in Anthropological Sciences from the University of New York at Stony Brook. He is also a much-acclaimed retreat master and provides spiritual direction to both Religious and the laity.

To partially fulfill the requirements for his doctorate, Fr. Mark spent a year in Egypt studying desert life and spirituality in Coptic monasteries. The results of his research are currently being considered for publication. Fr. Mark has lectured widely in his areas of research, both in professional and religious circles. In additional to his professional publications, he has also published articles in *Our Sunday Visitor,* the *Pittsburgh Catholic, New Covenant* and *Lay Witness.*

Sister M. Michele Ransil is a member of the Congregation of the Sisters of Divine Providence whose Motherhouse is located in Allison Park, Pennsylvania. She earned a B.E. and an M.A. in English from Duquesne University in Pittsburgh, an M.L.S. in Library Science from the University of Pittsburgh, and an M.A. in Executive Development for Public Service from Ball State University in Muncie, Indiana.

It was while working as a librarian at Ball State University in 1991 that Sr. Michele began to collaborate with Fr. Mark which resulted in the publication of their first book, *Wounded by Love.* Since her retirement from Ball State in June 1992, she has been working full time with Fr. Mark, transcribing, editing and formatting additional conferences for publication, as well as processing tapes from his local retreats for their tape ministry.